"Woodrow Kroll has written about the greatest subject—God. He also writes about man's greatest need—knowing God personally. This volume brings a warm and sympathetic heart and a bright scholastic mind together. It is designed and destined to help the reader to know God personally through understanding the Bible. I am happy to commend it fully."

ADRIAN ROGERS
SENIOR PASTOR
BELLEVUE BAPTIST CHURCH
MEMPHIS, TENNESSEE

"If you sincerely follow the principles Dr. Kroll shares in these pages, you will discover new excitement in Bible study and develop new enrichment in your daily fellowship with the Lord. Both new and experienced Bible students will find wise counsel and great encouragement in this book."

WARREN W. WIERSBE

"*How to Find God in the Bible* is relevant, from the futility of the *Matrix* and the Muslims in the first chapter to the final accessibility of God in the Bible in the last chapter."

PAUL R. HOLLINGER
OWNER/MANAGER WDAC/WBYN

How to Find God
in the Bible

HOW TO
FIND GOD
IN THE BIBLE

WOODROW KROLL

Multnomah® Publishers *Sisters, Oregon*

HOW TO FIND GOD IN THE BIBLE
published by Multnomah Publishers, Inc.

© 2004 by Woodrow Kroll
International Standard Book Number: 1-59052-256-7

Cover design by Design Concepts
Cover image by Jennifer Burrell/Masterfile

Italics in Scripture are the author's emphasis.
Unless otherwise indicated, Scripture quotations are from:
The Holy Bible, New International Version
© 1973, 1984 by International Bible Society,
used by permission of Zondervan Publishing House

Other Scripture quotations are from:
The Holy Bible, New King James Version (NKJV)
© 1984 by Thomas Nelson, Inc.
The Holy Bible, King James Version (KJV)
The New Testament in Modern English, Revised Edition (Phillips)
© 1958, 1960, 1972 by J. B. Phillips
Contemporary English Version (CEV) © 1995 by American Bible Society

Multnomah is a trademark of Multnomah Publishers, Inc.,
and is registered in the U.S. Patent and Trademark Office.
The colophon is a trademark of Multnomah Publishers, Inc.

Printed in the United States of America

For information:
MULTNOMAH PUBLISHERS, INC. • P.O. BOX 1720 • SISTERS, OR 97759

Library of Congress Cataloging-in-Publication Data

Kroll, Woodrow Michael, 1944-
  How to find God in the Bible / by Woodrow Kroll.
      p. cm.
  Includes bibliographical references.
  ISBN 1-59052-256-7 (pbk.)
  1. Christian life—Biblical teaching. 2. God—Biblical teaching. 3. God—
Knowableness—Biblical teaching. I. Title.

  BS680.C47K76 2004
  248.4—dc22

                                        2004000278

04 05 06 07 08 09—10 9 8 7 6 5 4 3 2 1 0

Dedicated to
Abe and Marj Van Der Puy
missionaries, statesmen,
examples for a whole generation to follow

CONTENTS

PART THREE
FOUR AMAZING BIBLE DISCOVERIES

ACKNOWLEDGMENTS

To effectively communicate how to connect with God through His Word, you need talented people helping you who have themselves connected with God. Such people have assisted me in writing this book.

My wife, Linda, has taught me much about God's desire to connect with me by modeling that desire in her love and life. Her own intimacy with God is an inspiration to me. I thank her for being an effective teacher.

Thanks, too, to Cathy Strate, my administrative assistant for more than two decades. She helped me find the time to work on this book and encouraged me throughout the process.

Allen Bean, head of the Biblical Communications Department at Back to the Bible, once again provided invaluable assistance in my research and editing.

Many thanks to Don Jacobson, president and publisher of Multnomah Publishers; to his marketing and sales staff, who worked hard to help this book find its readers; and to my capable editors—Thomas Womack, David Kopp, Jennifer Gott, and Steffany Woolsey.

Finally, I want to acknowledge those persons I've met or whose works I've read who have personally connected with God and taught me to do the same. I feel especially blessed. Thanks to all of you.

PREFACE

You and I have been on a quest for something. Like every other human, we search for significance, for inner peace, for spirituality,[1] for meaning in life. Life itself is a quest.

But God is on a quest too. His search will take Him to the ends of the earth and through all the corridors of time. And what, you might wonder, is God looking for?

God is on a quest for hearts—hearts that are also on a quest for Him. Jim Cymbala writes:

[God] is not looking for such things as knowledge or precious stones—after all, he knows everything and owns the world and everything in it. Although we rarely think about this or hear it preached, the Creator of all things is looking throughout the whole earth for a certain kind of heart. He is searching for a human heart that will allow him to show how marvelously he can strengthen, help, and bless someone's life.[2]

Take David. We know from the Bible that when the prophet
Samuel came to anoint David as Israel's next king, he found a
handsome, athletic young man. And we know David grew up to
be a great warrior and leader. But what impressed God most was
not his looks, his ability, his family, or his opportunities. It was
David's heart. God told Samuel, "Man looks at the outward
appearance, but the LORD looks at the heart" (1 Samuel 16:7).

Later, David revealed his heart when he wrote, "O God,
you are my God, earnestly I seek you; my soul thirsts for you,
my body longs for you, in a dry and weary land where there
is no water" (Psalm 63:1). Here David chose the verb *kahmahh*
to describe his physical longing for God. Used only here in the
Bible, the term is the equivalent of our modern expression, "If
I don't get that, I'll just die!"

David had a heart that longed to be close to God. And
God is still searching for that kind of heart today. In fact, God
wants to connect with you and me so much that He even ini-
tiates our thirst for Him. In his book *The Pursuit of God,* A. W.
Tozer wrote: "We pursue God because, and only because, He
has first put an urge within us that spurs us to the pursuit....
The impulse to pursue God originates with God, but the out-
working of that impulse is our following hard after Him."[3]

THE MEETING PLACE

If you sense that you are following hard after God, you might
be wondering where you can meet Him. Where can a seeking person go to meet God on a regular basis—day after
day—for a lifetime of intimacy with Him?

The answer is in the pages of His personal Message to you

and me, the Bible. Here is our connection with God. The Bible is the link between His heart and ours. The Bible is not simply a guide for life, a collection of wise sayings and wonderful stories. It is both the meeting place and the instrument that brings you and God together. As you become familiar with His Word, you can look forward to knowing God's heart for you.

That's what this book is about. It's about God, and you, and His Word. It's about the joy of discovering God and quenching your spiritual thirst through reading His Word.

Of course, many people read their Bibles for years without ever quenching their spiritual thirst. Somehow they have done the work but missed the benefit. They have seen the words but missed the Author.

But it doesn't have to be so!

The Bible says, "For the word of God is living and active. Sharper than any double-edged sword, it penetrates even to dividing soul and spirit, joints and marrow; it judges the thoughts and attitudes of the heart" (Hebrews 4:12). You see, not only does God promise to meet you in His Word, but He promises that you will discover the truths you've been looking for—about your world, your life, your self, and your God.

A THREE-PART INVITATION

This book is divided into three parts. The first part, "Prepare to Encounter God," focuses on how to prepare yourself to read your Bible for best results. We'll answer questions like, "How do I connect personally with God?" "How do I prepare myself for that encounter?" "How can I understand the

Bible and then put it to work in my life?"

The second part, "Why the Bible Can Change Your Life," shows the benefits of connecting with God through His Word. You'll answer the important question: "What benefits can I expect in my life when I read my Bible?"

The final part, "Four Amazing Bible Discoveries," explains the surprising and remarkable Bible truths that have revolutionized my life—and can do the same for you.

My sincere prayer is that every page that follows will help you on this, the most important quest of your life—your quest to meet and know God.

Woodrow Kroll

Lincoln, Nebraska

PART ONE

Prepare to
Encounter God

In the chapters that follow, you'll discover how to prepare yourself for your quest to connect with God. You'll learn that God has not been silent, but has purposefully and expectantly communicated with you. And you'll learn how to receive and understand that communication.

1 MAKE THE CONNECTION

Nobody ever outgrows Scripture;
the Book widens and deepens with our years.
—CHARLES HADDON SPURGEON

> ## IN THIS CHAPTER...
>
> ...find out how God connects with you.
>
> ...discover how you can connect with God.
>
> ...learn what you would not know about God without the Bible.

Thomas Anderson, a programmer for a leading software company, wanted answers. He wanted to connect with something beyond. Life didn't seem to be real. And then, as if by magic, his computer decided to start up a conversation with him.

Weird.

That led to a breathtaking and amazing ride. It was that ride, and the answers it sought, that had moviegoers lined up around the block just before the new millennium to see the futuristic film *The Matrix*.[1]

That blockbuster movie (and now its sequels) sought answers from everywhere, drawing from sources as diverse as the Bible, *Alice's Adventures in Wonderland,* Egyptian and Platonic traditions, and the teachings of the Gnostics. Most of all, the movie showed the influence of Zen Buddhism.

Here's the tragedy. Audiences were treated to wild and amazing special effects—but no answers. There was no connection with an almighty power. In fact, God was conspicuous by His absence.

Yet the majority of people around the world *do* believe in God. And they want to know: Does He have a personality? Is it possible to connect with Him? And if so, how?

Many look to media, or the arts, or the kind of hodge-podge spirituality of Hollywood for answers. But answers are hard to come by. That's not surprising. What is surprising is that even many religious traditions say, "No, you can't know God personally." In fact, for the majority of people of religious faith today, knowing God intimately isn't even an option.

Let me show you what I mean. Then you'll have a new appreciation for that Bible on your nightstand.

HOW RELIGIONS FAIL

Think about how major religious traditions approach connecting with God.

Muslims believe there is one almighty god named Allah, who is superior to mankind but quite distant. Allah is viewed as the creator of the universe and the source of both good and evil, but is not personally interested in the Muslims who worship him. Allah is a powerful and strict judge, too great to be approached by people. So for Muslims the idea of actually connecting with God is out of the question. It is impossible for people to have a relationship with Allah, or even to know much about him.

Hindus have an even more difficult time connecting with God. They worship a multitude of gods and goddesses, some three hundred thousand of them. Hindus believe that these diverse gods all converge into a universal spirit called the Ultimate Reality, or Brahman. But the Ultimate Reality is not a person, not knowable, and not at all loving. A Hindu's goal in life is to overcome the hardships of life through continuous and progressively higher reincarnations. Hinduism provides an explanation for suffering—the world is an evil place—but provides no loving God to offer an end to that suffering.

Buddhists do not worship any gods, so they have no incentive to get to know God. In fact, Buddhists believe that the universe operates by the principle of natural law, so they reject the notion of any supernatural power. Life is nothing but continuous pain, sorrow, and despair. Like Hindus, most Buddhists secretly believe that their hundreds of reincarnations only bring more misery. Buddhists meditate, but that's just a way to snuff out the flame of desire. Buddhists lack hope perhaps more than those of any other religious tradition.

The New Age movement promotes the development of the person's own power or divinity. When New Agers speak of God, they are not talking about a transcendent, personal God who created the universe. *They* are the only god there is, and the Earth is the source of all their spirituality. So to connect with God means to connect with yourself. That's not wrong, but it's ultimately not helpful enough either. For one thing, the "self" is one of our biggest problems. And for another, connecting with our "self" doesn't get us any closer to God.

The Christian tradition is different. Christians believe in a God who is a Person and has a personality, a God who created us, sustains our lives, loves us unconditionally, and wants to connect with us. We practice a faith that focuses on enjoying a relationship with God and becoming more connected to Him.

And what's even better, our faith—and the Bible on which it is founded—shows us how to do exactly that.

THE TRUTH ABOUT CONNECTING WITH GOD

The Bible shows us that our difficulty in knowing God personally arises from our sin, not from God's unwillingness to connect with us. As the prophet Isaiah observed, "Surely the arm of the LORD is not too short to save, nor his ear too dull to hear. But your iniquities have separated you from your God" (59:1–2). Until something is done about the guilt and penalty that accompanies our sin, no connectedness is possible. The chasm between God's holiness and our sinfulness is too great, and our ability to bridge it nonexistent.

Yet even though we could not come to God, He came to us—in the person of the Son of God, Jesus. "The Word became flesh and made his dwelling among us" (John 1:14); "The Son of Man came to seek and to save what was lost" (Luke 19:10). God connected with us in a way we least expected. He became a man and then died on the cross for us. Jesus paid a debt He didn't owe because we owed a debt we couldn't pay.

God is eager for you to connect with Him. "The LORD is near to all who call on him, to all who call on him in truth"

(Psalm 145:18). But connecting with God doesn't happen through the Eight Fold Path, the Five Pillars, meditation, doing good works, or reciting the Christian creeds. Connection with God comes as a result of a relationship with God through faith in His Son, Jesus Christ: "Believe in the Lord Jesus, and you will be saved" (Acts 16:31).

It's when you read the Bible that God reveals Himself and His eternal plan for your salvation.

OUR GOD IS NOT SILENT

The God of the Bible is not a silent god. In fact, He has been quite communicative with us. The expression "And God said" or "Then God said" occurs nine times in the first chapter of the Bible. "God blessed them and said" is found once. The Bible begins with God talking—speaking creation into existence.

God also chose to speak directly with people. Here are some examples from Scripture:

PEOPLE WITH WHOM GOD SPOKE DIRECTLY	
PERSON	SCRIPTURE CITATION
Adam	Genesis 1:28–29; 2:16
Eve	Genesis 3:13, 16
Cain	Genesis 4:6, 9, 15
Noah	Genesis 6:13; 7:1; 9:12, 17
Abraham	Genesis 13:14; 17:9, 15; 18:13, 20
Sarah	Genesis 18:15
Jacob	Genesis 31:3; 35:1, 10–11
Rebekah	Genesis 25:23

Person	Scripture Citation
Aaron	Exodus 4:27; 6:26; Numbers 18:1
Balaam	Numbers 22:12
Joshua	Joshua 3:7; 5:2; 6:2; 10:8; 13:1
Israel	Judges 1:2; 2:1; 1 Kings 11:2
Gideon	Judges 6:16, 23, 25; 7:2, 4, 5–7, 9
Samuel	1 Samuel 3:11; 8:7, 22; 9:17; 16:1–2, 12
David	1 Samuel 23:2; 2 Samuel 2:1; 1 Kings 8:18
Solomon	1 Kings 9:3; 11:11; 2 Kings 21:7
Ahijah	1 Kings 14:5, 7
Elijah	1 Kings 17:14; 19:9; 2 Chronicles 21:12
Micaiah	1 Kings 22:17, 20, 22; 2 Chronicles 18:16, 19
Elisha	2 Kings 9:6
Jehu	2 Kings 10:30
Huldah the prophetess	2 Kings 22:15–16, 18
Josiah	2 Kings 23:27
Shemaiah	2 Chronicles 11:2–4
Eliphaz the Temanite	Job 42:7
Isaiah	Isaiah 8:1; 18:4; 2 Kings 19:20
Jeremiah	Jeremiah 1:7, 9; 2:19; 3:6; 15:11; 23:2; 30:2
Ezekiel	Ezekiel 2:4; 3:27; 5:5, 7–8, 11
Hosea	Hosea 1:2, 4, 6
Amos	Amos 3:13; 7:1, 4, 7–8, 15
Obadiah	Obadiah 1:1
Jonah	Jonah 4:9

God also spoke with people through the angels who occa-
sionally acted as divine spokesmen. At times the appearance of
the angel of the Lord in the Old Testament is Christ Himself.

PEOPLE WITH WHOM GOD SPOKE THROUGH ANGELS	
PERSON	SCRIPTURE CITATION
Abraham	Genesis 22:11, 15
Hagar	Genesis 16:7–11
Balaam	Numbers 22:32, 35
Israel	Judges 2:1, 4
Deborah and Barak	Judges 5:23
Gideon	Judges 6:12
Hannah	Judges 13:3
Manoah	Judges 13:13, 16, 18
Elijah	2 Kings 1:3–4, 15

Sometimes God spoke with Himself, one Person of the
Godhead speaking to the other Persons (Genesis 1:26; 3:22;
8:21–22; 11:6–7). Sometimes He spoke to no one in particular (Genesis 2:18; 6:3, 7; 18:17). And what may surprise you
the most, God sometimes even spoke directly with His arch-
enemy—Satan (Job 1:7–8, 12; 2:2–3, 6; Zechariah 3:2).

When God Speaks to People

The Lord spoke often with His prophets, telling them what
to say to kings and commoners, especially His people Israel.
A rather obscure prophet named Micaiah reminded King

Ahab's messenger: "As surely as the LORD lives, I can tell him only what the LORD tells me" (1 Kings 22:14). Sometimes God just directed the prophet's mind through a vision or an overpowering visitation of God's Spirit to communicate with them (2 Chronicles 15:1). In fact, this is how God communicated to forty different authors what He wanted included in His written Word, the Bible. "For prophecy never had its origin in the will of man, but men spoke from God as they were carried along by the Holy Spirit" (2 Peter 1:21).

The person with whom God talked most often—directly, personally, intimately—was Moses: "The LORD would speak to Moses face to face, as a man speaks with his friend" (Exodus 33:11). So special was the connection between God and Moses that Deuteronomy 34:10 says, "Since then, no prophet has risen in Israel like Moses, whom the LORD knew face to face." More than seventy-five times the Bible records God talking with Moses.[2]

God appears to be almost chatty in the Old Testament. But what about the New Testament?

As far as I know, the only reference to God speaking directly with someone is in Jesus' parable of the rich fool. Jesus said, "But God said to him, 'You fool! This very night your life will be demanded from you. Then who will get what you have prepared for yourself?'" (Luke 12:20).

Why such a talkative God in the Old Testament and so little chatter in the New Testament? Because in the New Testament, God didn't have to do much talking for Himself. God the Son came, among other reasons, to speak on the Father's behalf. Often Jesus said things like, "For I did not speak of my own accord, but the Father who sent me commanded me what to say and how to say it.... So whatever I say is just what the Father has told me to say" (John 12:49–50; see also 8:28, 38; 14:10).

"In the past God spoke to our forefathers," says the writer of Hebrews, "through the prophets at many times and in various ways, but in these last days he has spoken to us by his Son, whom he appointed heir of all things, and through whom he made the universe" (Hebrews 1:1–2).

When first-century seekers heard the words of Jesus, they were hearing God speak. When you and I read the words of Jesus, we hear God too.

What About Today?

But what about now? Why doesn't He speak in an audible voice now? He doesn't need to. Now God speaks through His Word. That's what Jesus said. "These words you hear are not my own; they belong to the Father who sent me. All this I have spoken while still with you. But the Counselor, the Holy Spirit, whom the Father will send in my name, will teach you all things and will remind you of everything I have said to you" (John 14:24–26). When you read the Word of God, the Spirit of God uses all that Jesus said and what God recorded in His Word to connect you with the Almighty.

Perhaps you have gone backpacking in the Rockies or trekking in the Alps and felt especially close to God as you breathed the cool mountain air and drank in the beauty around you. Everything in God's creation speaks to you about Him. "The heavens declare the glory of God; the skies proclaim the work of his hands" (Psalm 19:1). But if you rely only on nature to connect with God, you will not experience the full relationship God intends you to have. Nature alone will not make the connection you seek. Hymn writer Isaac Watts understood this when he wrote:

> The heavens declare Thy glory, Lord,
>   In every star Thy wisdom shines;
> But when our eyes behold Thy Word,
>   We read Thy name in fairer lines.

WITHOUT A BIBLE...

There is much about God that you would never know apart from His Word. Sure, you may become convinced that God exists by what you see in the world. You may even philosophically come to the conclusion that the order in our universe demands an almighty Creator to bring it about. But if the Bible had never been written, think about all the things you would never know about God.

Without a Bible, you would never know that "God so loved the world that he gave his one and only Son, that whoever believes in him shall not perish but have eternal life" (John 3:16).

Without a Bible, you would never know that God "will keep him in perfect peace, whose mind is stayed on You, because he trusts in You" (Isaiah 26:3, NKJV).

Without a Bible, you would never know that "the eyes of the LORD range throughout the earth to strengthen those whose hearts are fully committed to him" (2 Chronicles 16:9).

Without a Bible, you would never know that "those who

hope in the LORD will renew their strength. They will soar on wings like eagles; they will run and not grow weary, they will walk and not be faint" (Isaiah 40:31).

Without a Bible, you would never know that God takes no pleasure in punishing sinners: "Do I take any pleasure in the death of the wicked? declares the Sovereign LORD. Rather, am I not pleased when they turn from their ways and live?" (Ezekiel 18:23).

Without a Bible, you would never hear Jesus' invitation: "Come to me, all you who are weary and burdened, and I will give you rest" (Matthew 11:28).

Without a Bible, you would never understand that "the wages of sin is death, but the gift of God is eternal life in Christ Jesus our Lord" (Romans 6:23).

Without a Bible, you would never realize that "salvation is found in no one else, for there is no other name under heaven given to men by which we must be saved," but the name Jesus (Acts 4:12).

Without a Bible, you would never know that "there is one God and one mediator between God and men, the man Christ Jesus, who gave himself as a ransom for all men" (1 Timothy 2:5–6).

Without a Bible, you would not have God's promise that "all things work together for good to those who love God, to those who are the called according to His purpose" (Romans 8:28, NKJV).

Without a Bible, you would not appreciate that "if anyone is in Christ, he is a new creation; the old has gone, the new has come!" (2 Corinthians 5:17).

Without a Bible, you would not recognize that "it is by

grace you have been saved, through faith—and this not from yourselves, it is the gift of God" (Ephesians 2:8).

Without a Bible, you would never guess that a day is coming when God "will wipe every tear from their eyes. There will be no more death or mourning or crying or pain, for the old order of things has passed away" (Revelation 21:4).

Without a Bible, you would not be encouraged, "Behold, I am coming soon! My reward is with me, and I will give to everyone according to what he has done. I am the Alpha and the Omega, the First and the Last, the Beginning and the End" (Revelation 22:12–13).

Without a Bible, you would know very little about God, His character, His promises and plans for you, or what awaits you in the future. All this and more is revealed only through the pages of His Word. If you want to encounter God and His truth, becoming one with nature just isn't enough.

FINDING A PERSON, FINDING HOME

As a tether connects an astronaut to his shuttle, so God's Word connects you to the Almighty. To encounter Him, you have to spend time in His Word. That's your point of connection. That's what brings you home to God.

Look at these statements from the Bible, which put its benefits in perspective:

- "Your word is a lamp to my feet and a light for my path" (Psalm 119:105). The Bible connects you to God's way.

- "How can a young man keep his way pure? By living according to your word" (Psalm 119:9). The Bible connects you to God's holiness.
- "Man shall not live by bread alone, but by every word of God" (Luke 4:4, NKJV). The Bible connects you to God's life.
- "For you have been born again, not of perishable seed, but of imperishable, through the living and enduring word of God" (1 Peter 1:23). The Bible connects you to God's eternity.
- "Sanctify them by the truth; your word is truth" (John 17:17). The Bible connects you to God's truth.
- "Faith comes by hearing, and hearing by the word of God" (Romans 10:17, NKJV).

You see, the Bible connects you to God Himself. In the other world religions you may find inspiration, rituals, or traditions. But in Christianity, you discover a relationship with a Person who *has spoken*. He is compassionate, merciful, and forgiving. And His Word provides more than just a spiritual path or philosophy.

It brings you the very words of Life—and brings you to the One who wants you to receive them.

2

THE MEETING PLACE

*The hardest part of a missionary career
is to maintain regular, prayerful Bible study.*

—J. HUDSON TAYLOR

IN THIS CHAPTER...

...determine the right time to go after God.

...isolate the right place to go after God.

...identify the right tools to go after God.

The clock says 5:59 A.M. In just sixty seconds, Jim will be up and within an hour on his way to the health club. It's part of his daily routine. "I wouldn't miss it. I feel better, think better, work better, play harder," says Jim, "when I hit the health club every morning." His workout regimen prepares him for a good day ahead.

But first Jim prepares himself spiritually. How does he do that? In many of the same ways he prepares himself physically. As soon as that alarm goes off, he gets up, brushes his teeth, and sits in his usual spot to spend some quality time with God.

He has a routine, and he tries to stick with it. Why? Because he gets results.

I want to share with you from my own spiritual preparation routine. If you're struggling to get connected with God through His Word, maybe what I've learned will help you. There's nothing magical or superspiritual about these things, but they work.

Here's what I do:

GO AFTER GOD EARLY

The psalmist wrote: "In the morning, O LORD, you hear my voice; in the morning I lay my requests before you and wait in expectation" (Psalm 5:3). If you want to connect with God, set aside the first part of your day.

Not everybody can do this of course, but I go after God early for three reasons.

First, early in my day is when I have the fewest distractions. It's when I have the best opportunity to focus on God. It's also when my heart is least encumbered with the difficulties of the day. My relationship with God is the most important relationship in my life. It deserves to be my first priority every day.

Second, I need spiritual nourishment early—before I start my day. Your mother always told you that breakfast is the most important meal of the day. Why wouldn't a morning breakfast with God be your most important spiritual meal of the day? Jesus said, "Seek first his kingdom and his righteousness, and all these things will be given to you as well" (Matthew 6:33). My day is too demanding to begin it with anything other than kingdom business. If I don't start there, the other business of my life will tend to defeat me and overrun what must come first.

Third, I've noticed that in Bible times, God often took action "early in the morning" (see Genesis 22:13; Exodus 8:20; 9:13; Joshua 6:12; Mark 16:2). I want to connect with God during the part of my day when I know His Spirit is very active.

But no matter what time I rise to meet Him, I find Him already waiting for me. Meeting God early clears the clutter out of my life and prepares me for the challenges I will encounter that day. Here's how I express that in verse:

Early in the morning
    I rise to meet the Lord,
He makes His presence known to me
    Through the pages of His Word.
For when I meet Him early
    At the dawning of the day,
The hours go more smoothly
    Whatever comes my way.
But if I fail to meet Him
    And rush to other things,
I face the kind of failures
    That a day without Him brings.
So here's a little secret
    To make your day go right,
Meet God early in the morning
    And praise Him every night.[1]

You might be thinking, *That's good for you, but I'm not an early riser.* That's okay. *Early* is a relative word. John Wesley made it his habit to rise about 4:30 A.M. to spend uninterrupted time with the Lord. But you don't have to do what Wesley did. What's early for you may be different from what's early for me. Just make it a practice to give God your best time, and you'll discover that your days go much better.

FIND THE RIGHT MEETING PLACE

You can connect with God anywhere, but there are always special places where God's people meet with Him. Where's your special place?

When I was in college, my major was General Languages. That meant I had to have a two-year sequence of at least three different languages. I studied French, German, Spanish, Latin, Greek, and Hebrew *all at the same time.* Needless to say, this became a bit confusing. Then I hit upon a plan.

I would study French in one chair in the living room, Greek at the table in the kitchen, German on the couch, Hebrew in the den…you get the idea. A special spot was used for each language. When I took an exam I would mentally put myself back in that chair or at that table. The familiarity of the site helped me be more familiar with each language. It sounds simple, but it worked.

For me, my special place to meet with God is at my desk in the study of our home. My wife, Linda, and I have our family devotions in the family room every night after dinner. But my personal quiet time with the Lord is done in *my* chair, at *my* desk, in *my* room.

The place where you meet with God should be a quiet place. Jesus sought quiet, out-of-the-way places to meet with His heavenly Father. I encourage you to do the same (I'll have more to say about this in the next chapter). Wherever your special place is, finding the right spot to connect with God is similar to how a little boy described an elevator: "I got into this little room and the upstairs came down."

When you find your own place to read His Word, God will come down and meet you there.

BRING THE RIGHT TOOLS

Every time Linda asks me to do something around the house, before I promise her anything, I check to see if I have the right tools. You don't need a lot of fancy study tools to get the most out of your time with God. But some tools have proved consistently useful for generations of Bible students. Here are a few suggestions:

You need a Bible.

Not just any Bible—your Bible. One you feel comfortable with. Pick a version you like to read, one you can understand. Some have a favorite version and they stick with it. That's fine. I have a favorite version too, but I often read a variety of versions to enhance my understanding and to be aware of how different versions treat a passage.[2]

By the way, make sure your version isn't in a type size that leaves you struggling to read. All of my Bibles are now giant print. I'm okay with that.

You need a spiritual journal.

This can be a plain spiral-bound notebook, a personal journal, or a computer program. What you use depends on your preferences and your pocketbook. But whatever you decide, use something. Unlike a diary, a spiritual journal is for the single purpose of giving you a place to record what you're learning, note favorite verses, and write out prayers.

Think about it: If you ask God to speak to you and you don't have some way to record what He impresses on your mind, you'll be much less likely to remember and act on it. Also, a journal allows you to look back and see how God has been working in your life over a period of time. Next to your Bible, a spiritual journal may be the most important tool to help you grow in your personal relationship with God.

You may need a concordance.

A concordance is simply an alphabetical listing of every word found in the Bible, with the reference where it is found.[3] So if you encounter a word in your reading that you remember seeing elsewhere, but you just can't remember where, look it up in your Bible concordance. Today you can get a concordance for almost every translation of the Bible. Many are now available on CD-ROM.[4]

You may need a Bible dictionary.

A Bible dictionary explains the meanings of the major words found in the Bible.[5] It can be especially helpful when you need to know the meaning of an unfamiliar word before you read on. A Bible dictionary can help you keep straight the difference between an ephah and an ephod; between Herodias, Herodion, Herodium, and the Herodians…and a whole lot more.

Bible maps will keep you from getting "lost."

Most Christians don't know much about Bible geography.[6] Maps not only show you where cities, mountains, lakes, and seas are located; they also show the relative distances between them. Topographical maps (maps that show elevation) can clarify phrases like the one in the story of the good Samaritan: "A man was going down from Jerusalem to Jericho" (Luke 10:30). A map shows Jericho northeast of Jerusalem and ordinarily you would say the man went "up" to Jericho. But a topographical map shows that Jerusalem is 2700 feet above sea level and Jericho, just a short seventeen miles away, is almost 900 feet *below* sea level. The man was definitely going "down" from Jerusalem to Jericho.

A one-volume Bible commentary can provide good teaching.

A Bible commentary—a scholar's explanation of a text—can help you understand a difficult passage or allow you to compare your interpretation with an expert.[7]

Still, your best learning will come from self-discovery. That's why I recommend that you not read a commentary on a passage before you read the passage yourself and spend time thinking and praying about it. The same Holy Spirit who teaches the experts teaches you. Granted, the experts may have more training and background in the original languages, in theology, and in history. But make sure you are looking for God first in His Word, not in someone else's commentary. Read the Bible for yourself. Then ask the Holy Spirit to guide you into truth.

KEEP OUT ALL DISTRACTIONS

If you are going to devote yourself to seeking God during a specific time each day, you will need to close out all other distractions. That's easier said than done, I know, but God isn't into timesharing.

In his helpful little book *Adrenalin and Stress*, Archibald Hart talks about relaxing so you can read God's Word and meditate on it. He gives this somewhat direct advice on closing out all distractions: "Ensure you won't be interrupted. Lock the door, hang out a sign, tell spouse, kids, and neighbors not to disturb you or go where they can't find you. Unplug the telephone and make sure the stove is off."[8]

Linda and I started having family devotions early in our marriage. Then our children came along and they joined in. When they became teenagers, they understood that during our family time with God, no one was to disturb us. If the phone rang, we didn't answer it. If there was a knock at the door, we figured they would come back. Nothing, absolutely nothing, was allowed to infringe on our time with God.

I have followed that same practice in my personal time. No instant messages, no e-mail, no phones, no entry. This is my time with God and interruptions are strictly prohibited. Think about how you feel when you're talking with someone on the phone and you know they're carrying on a conversation with someone else. I think that's how God must feel when we don't keep distractions out while we're meeting with Him.

BE PREPARED FOR ANYTHING

The Bible is the most unique book in all the world. Read Michael Crichton or Mary Higgins Clark and you will be entertained, but not necessarily enriched. Read Tom Clancy or Agatha Christie and you will be entranced, but will your life be changed? Probably not. But read the Bible and you will be entertained, enriched, and entranced—and most of all changed. No other book even dares to make the claim to be alive, living, and life-changing—but the Bible does (Hebrews 4:12). Every time you read the Bible, you should be prepared for anything. You never know what will happen.

Consider the ancient story of King Josiah. Judah had been under decades of leadership by ungodly kings when Josiah came to the throne. In the eighteenth year of his reign, King Josiah decided to rebuild the temple, which his grandfather had profaned. During the process, Hilkiah the high priest came across the Book of the Law, which hadn't been read in years. Shaphan the scribe read from the Law in the king's presence, and Josiah tore his regal robes in shame at the Jews' neglect of God's Word. Because the reading of the Word humbled Josiah so greatly, a great revival ensued.

Josiah rid Judah of the trappings of paganism, and the people were completely changed. The Bible says, "Neither before nor after Josiah was there a king like him who turned to the LORD as he did—with all his heart and with all his soul and with all his strength" (2 Kings 23:25).

As you approach God's Word each day, prepare for refreshment. Prepare for the exact insight you'll need in the day ahead. Prepare to experience God's presence. Prepare for your life to change in the most surprising ways!

3 THE TAPESTRY OF DEVOTION

Speed-reading may be a good thing but it was never meant for the Bible. It takes calm, thoughtful, prayerful meditation on the Word to extract its deepest nourishment.

—VANCE HAVNER

IN THIS CHAPTER...

...learn how to spend time talking with God.

...learn how to read the Bible devotionally.

...learn how to "marinate" your mind with God's truth.

Several years ago, while I was visiting churches in northern Italy, a local pastor took me to the town square in Milan. In the shops there I found an authentic Italian tapestry. It was an exquisite example of detail and craftsmanship and it was within my price range, so I decided to buy it.

Just as I was about to begin the bargaining process, I turned the tapestry over. That's when I noticed that it was even more beautiful than I had thought. You see, I had been looking at the reverse side of the tapestry. Once I turned it around and viewed it "right side up," I saw just how breathtaking it really was!

I like to think of my daily devotional time with God as four precious strands woven together like a fine tapestry. The four strands are: a time to pray, a time to read, a time to write about what I've read, and a time to think.

Let's take a closer look.

A TIME TO PRAY

Prayer is your ongoing conversation with God. In prayer you worship God, tell Him how you feel and what you're concerned about, confess sin, make your requests, listen for His answers, and give Him your thanks. In prayer you talk personally and honestly. You acknowledge who God is and who you are. You connect with God's heart by laying bare your own.

Begin by focusing on Him.

My personal morning time with God begins with what I call my "Hello Lord, it's me again" prayer. It's okay to ask God for things you need: "You do not have because you do not ask" (James 4:2, NKJV). In fact, I encourage you to use the ACTS formula (Adoration, Confession, Thanksgiving, and Supplication) to bring balance in your prayer life. But first thing in the morning, it's best to concentrate on the first two, maybe the first three parts of the ACTS formula. It helps me to spend the first five minutes just recalling God's names, His attributes, His character, His promises, His plans for me. I find that it's a good time to quote the psalms I've memorized.

Do a heart-and-hands check.

Since this is the beginning of my day, I want to start out right with the Lord. Morning is the best time to face the thoughts, attitudes, and actions in your life that are wrong and need God's cleansing and forgiveness (Psalm 24:3–4).

Think of your mind and life as your computer, which is constantly storing data—some you want, some you don't. The files that slow down your connection with God need to be purged on a regular basis. Some files in your life—thoughts, images, actions—require constant hitting of the delete key. That's confession.

When I meet God in the morning, I prepare my heart by deleting all the junk mail that has been accumulating in my mind and heart. In fact, I try to do this every time I pray to God throughout the day. I don't want to get overloaded with the spiritual spam of Satan. The Bible promises, "If we confess our sins, he is faithful and just and will forgive us our sins and purify us from all unrighteousness" (1 John 1:9).

Ask for the expert Counselor.

Have you ever been told that you need professional help? Well, you do. A professional is one who engages in a pursuit or activity with special expertise. As you enter the pages of Scripture, your expert Counselor is the Holy Spirit. Jesus told His disciples that after He left, the Holy Spirit would come to help and guide, leading all Christ's followers into the truth (John 14:16, 26).

The following chart reveals the numerous ways the Holy Spirit gives "professional" help.

What the Holy Spirit Does for the Christian

The Holy Spirit *regenerates* the Christian
TITUS 3:5–6

The Holy Spirit *baptizes* the Christian
GALATIANS 3:27–28

The Holy Spirit *indwells* the Christian
JOHN 14:16–17

The Holy Spirit *seals* the Christian
EPHESIANS 1:13; 4:30

The Holy Spirit *anoints* the Christian
1 JOHN 2:20, 27

The Holy Spirit *prays* for the Christian
ROMANS 8:26–27

The Holy Spirit *convicts* the Christian
1 JOHN 3:20

The Holy Spirit *confirms* the Christian
ROMANS 8:16

The Holy Spirit *teaches* the Christian
1 JOHN 2:27

The Holy Spirit *guides* the Christian
ROMANS 8:14

The Holy Spirit *sanctifies* the Christian
2 CORINTHIANS 3:18

The Holy Spirit *fills* the Christian
EPHESIANS 5:18

The Holy Spirit *gifts* the Christian
1 CORINTHIANS 12:1–31

The Holy Spirit *renews* the Christian
ROMANS 12:1–2

When you begin to connect with God through reading His Word, you don't have to tackle the challenge alone. You can ask for help, professional help—the help of the Holy Spirit.

Ask God to touch you.

Yes, the Bible has special meaning for its first readers. And yes, God has been changing lives through His Word for centuries. But be sure to ask God to use His Word to impact *you*—your life, your needs, your desires—today.

When you realize—and experience—that God's Word was written for you, your connection with Him will flourish. Until then the Bible is of little more value than a literary masterpiece.

So ask God to impress something special on your heart and soul from what you read. Ask Him to change a little part of you through His Word. Ask God to make Himself so real to you that you will be a different person when you walk out into your day.

A TIME TO READ

You speak with God through prayer; God speaks with you through His Word. So while prayer prepares me to meet the real God, reading His Word is when He actually shows me His heart.

How can you and I get the most out of this reading experience?

Read devotionally.

There are lots of productive ways to read the Bible.

- You can read God's Word *systematically*—a specific portion every day.
- You can read God's Word *topically*—looking for parallel passages that teach parallel truths.
- You can read God's Word *progressively*—reading together those portions that are linked by a particular thought.
- You can read the Bible one book at a time.[1]

There is benefit to all these approaches. Whatever plan you use, if your intent is to get to know God better, learn how to read His letter to you *devotionally*.

When you read your Bible devotionally, you take things personally. Why? You want to connect with God one-on-one. Your reading is an expression of devotion to Him. You sincerely want to know not just the content of God's Word, but its Author.

So instead of stopping at understanding the content of a passage, you pay special attention to clues given about the Person doing the writing. For example, you might look for words and phrases that reveal God's emotions—love, joy, sorrow, grief, or commitment. Then soak up their meaning as if you were a sponge, and apply their insights to your relationship with Him.

When you come to an especially tender passage, such as, "I have loved you with an everlasting love" (Jeremiah 31:3), or "I have engraved you on the palms of my hands" (Isaiah 49:16), pause and receive its meaning for you today. Stop and say, "Oooh! Look at that!" It's the intimacy equivalent of stopping to smell the roses.

Because devotional reading is such a personal quest, you should pay special attention to passages that reveal God's character; His purposes and priorities; His record of actions, desires, and commands; and His promises to everyone (including you).

Read with all your senses.

Dr. Elmer Towns focuses on this truth in his book *A Beginner's Guide to Reading the Bible.*[2] He tells about his uncle Sam (he really does have an uncle named Sam!) sitting on the front porch of his South Carolina farm telling stories. To make sure all the kids paid attention, Uncle Sam would say, "Listen with your eyes." As strange as that sounds, Uncle Sam wanted the kids to listen to his story with all their senses, not just their ears. We should read the Bible the same way—with more than just one of our senses.

Dr. Towns says you must first read with your ears—that is, read aloud.[3] When Philip encountered the Ethiopian eunuch, he "ran up to the chariot and heard the man reading Isaiah the prophet" (Acts 8:30). He was reading with his ears. Then you must read with your mouth, that is, get a good "taste" for what the words are saying. Next read with your nose. Breathe deeply every time you read of fresh fish, newly baked bread, or lamb cooking in a stew. Smell what you read. Also read with your touch, imagining that your hands are holding the objects or brushing over the surfaces of what you're reading about. Finally, read with your eyes, allowing the rich visual experiences of the Bible to enter your imagination.

Read and reread.

When I was a little boy growing up in the hills of western Pennsylvania, my father took special delight in telling my older brother and me this little ditty: "Pete and Repeat went down to the river to swim. Pete fell in. Who was left?" When we would naively say, "Repeat," he would continue, "Pete and Repeat went down to the river to swim...." Strange as it may seem, that comes back to me often when I am spending time in God's Word.

Reading a passage once is insufficient to grasp the full depth of the passage. Famed Bible expositor G. Campbell Morgan never preached on any book of the Bible until he had first read it out loud fifty times.[4] If you don't feel like you've become intimate enough with God after one reading, do what you would do if you received a letter from the love of your life. Read it again, and again.

A TIME TO WRITE

There is a positive connection between writing and remembering. If you take the time to write down some of the things God impresses upon you while you are reading His Word, your chances of remembering them and making them your own increase exponentially. Here are some ways to do that.

Mark your Bible.

Sometimes when I suggest that people mark important things in the margins of their Bible, I receive a recoiling look of horror. "What? Write in the Sacred Text?" I understand their concern. The Word of God must be respected. But reverence and worship are not the same. I reverence the book, but I worship the God who wrote the book. I mark in my Bible because it helps me be more familiar with it and more intimate with its Author.

In my many Bibles over the years I have written hundreds of notes and personal discoveries. I date those discoveries. I look back at the notes I wrote forty years ago and say, "Well, duh, everybody knows that." But I was just discovering it at the time. I never give away any of my Bibles because they are a chronological record of my own spiritual growth. They are a treasure to me.

Make personal notes.

In 1970, I was a student at the University of Strasbourg, France. In one of my classes the professor strolled in, sat down, and began to read his lecture, head down, face buried in his notes. Every student but me got up from their seats and assembled in the back of the room. Soon all but one left. When class was over, I asked the other remaining student where they had gone. He told me the final exam was our only grade in the class and he was elected to take notes. He would copy them and sell copies to the others. They would return to class on the day of the final.

I have on my shelf multiple volumes of personal notes I've taken while reading my Bible. They will never be published, and they probably aren't important to anyone but me. But they were my discoveries in journeying through God's Word. I'm sure somebody made those same discoveries before me, but I enjoyed the trip just the same. (Captain James Cook got to

Hawaii before me too, but that didn't stop me from enjoying a vacation there!)

What kinds of discoveries are in my personal notes? Verses I found especially meaningful. Texts I want to come back to and preach on someday. Lists that interest me—for example, all the "I am" passages, the altars built in the Bible, unusual names, people whose names God changed, and more. But most of my notes focus on issues of the heart—things about God that I appreciate so deeply and understand so superficially. These notes record where God's heart touched my life. They will be forever precious to me. Your notes will be precious to you too.

A TIME TO THINK

It's thick. It's juicy. It's still sizzling on the grill. And it's for you. I'm talking about pure 100 percent Nebraska corn-fed beef.

But there's more. Your delicious steak wasn't just unwrapped and thrown on the grill. Oh no. It was marinated in a savory sauce of herbs and spices—marinated, in fact, for two days. When it hit the grill, the juices fell from the meat to the charcoal below and fired the flames, giving your steak that "just right" look. Trust me. This is going to be the best steak you've ever tasted....

Okay, you're hungry now. Admit it. You can smell that steak grilling, can't you?

I just did to your mind what the chef did to your steak. I marinated it. I made you think about that steak. And the more you thought about it, the more you could see the juices, hear the sizzle, smell the aroma. That's what thinking about what you read does for your connection with God.

When you meditate on what you've read in God's Word, you soak up Bible truth. You let it marinate your gray matter. That's how truth sinks deep into your mind and heart—and becomes completely yours.

I had been keeping my appointment with God every morning for many years before I understood the truth of this. My habit had been to pray for a half hour, read God's Word for a half hour, then say a quick "good-bye" prayer and get on with my busy day.

But I began to feel that something was missing. Then I hit on a plan. Instead of dividing my morning time with God in half—praying and reading—I would divide it in thirds:

- pray for twenty minutes,
- read and write for twenty minutes, and
- do nothing for twenty minutes.

That's right, do nothing. I would just wait on the Lord. I would take time to think about what I had read. I would let my encounter with God's Word "marinate" my mind.

And it worked. I felt new intimacy with my heavenly Father and new spiritual strength. The Bible says, "Those who wait on the LORD shall renew their strength" (Isaiah 40:31, NKJV).

My "do nothing" plan is simple. There are three essential elements: *solitude*—I wait singly; *stillness*—I wait tranquilly; and *silence*—I wait quietly. For me, meditating turned out to be the missing piece of the puzzle. It has been in those final tranquil moments that intimacy with God really happens.

Look more closely at the three *Ss* with me:

Solitude

My wife has four sisters and two brothers. While we were dating, I was in college and she was back in the town where we
grew up. When I came home, I would visit with almost all her
siblings, but it was with Linda that I wanted to spend time. Her
two younger sisters, Kathy and Jodi, who were five and three
at the time, loved to climb up on my knee. But I couldn't
exactly build intimacy with Linda while entertaining her sisters. What we needed was time alone.

Time alone together is vital for any close, growing relationship. Jesus walked on water and then sent the amazed
crowds away. Why? Matthew 14:23 says, "After he had dismissed them, he went up on a mountainside by himself to
pray." On another occasion, "Very early in the morning, while
it was still dark, Jesus got up, left the house and went off to a
solitary place, where he prayed" (Mark 1:35).

A favorite hymn beautifully captures the intimacy that
comes when we shut others out and spend time alone with
God.

> I come to the garden alone,
>   while the dew is still on the roses.
> And the voice I hear, falling on my ear,
>   the Son of God discloses.
> And He walks with me and He talks with me,
>   and He tells me I am His own.
> And the joy we share, as we tarry there;
>   none other has ever known.

Stillness

When I came home from college to see Linda, we were usually busy. We went to amusement parks. We attended church and youth group. Even when we were alone we were busy, always on the go. But we discovered that to really get to know each other, we needed quiet time alone. You need that same stillness as you wait before God after reading His Word. A. W. Tozer wrote about the losses that come when we neglect stillness with God:

> Failure to see this [the need to be still before God] is the cause of a very serious breakdown in modern evangelicalism....We read our chapter, have our short devotions and rush away, hoping to make up for our deep inward bankruptcy by attending another gospel meeting or listening to another thrilling story told by a religious adventurer lately returned from afar. The tragic results of this spirit are all about us: Shallow lives, hollow religious philosophies...the glorification of men...the mistaking of dynamic personally for the power of the Spirit. These and such are the symptoms of an evil disease, a deep and serious malady of the soul.[5]

If you're having difficulty connecting with God, maybe you need to change your approach. Don't try to get to know God only in a group. Shut out your world for a time each day and sit in stillness before Him. God tells us in His Word, "Be still, and know that I am God" (Psalm 46:10).

Silence

As Linda and I grew closer, we often spent time just gazing into each other's eyes. We hardly needed to talk. Our love was growing and young love has a language all its own. Each day we grew closer and closer.

In your time with God, be sure to make time for silence. Don't pray anything, say anything, or write or read anything. Just quietly, reverently be *with* Him. Show Him that you simply love His presence. Your silent actions will speak much louder than your words and will move you closer to His heart.

A TAPESTRY OF JOY

Recently I visited the buildings in Bristol, England, where George Mueller operated his orphanage many years ago. Mueller was a remarkable man of faith. He had a connection with God that many only dream about. What was the secret of that connection?

In Mueller's own words:

> I saw more clearly than ever, that the first great and primary business to which I ought to attend every day was to have a soul happy in the Lord. The first thing to be concerned about was not how much I might serve the Lord, how I might glorify the Lord; but how I might get my soul into a happy state, and how my inner man may be nourished.... I saw that the most important thing I had to do was to give myself to the reading of the Word of God and to meditation on it.[6]

A happy soul is one that is filled with the joy of the Lord, one prepared as well-tilled soil, to receive whatever the Lord has for you. And the elements of devotion we've been talking about—time to pray, read, write, and meditate—are the threads of my spiritual tapestry of joy.

4

How to Relate to the Bible

*If God gives you a watch, are you honoring Him
more by asking Him what time it is
or by simply consulting the watch?*

—A. W. Tozer

In this chapter...

...become familiar
with the
"landscape" of the
Bible.

...get to know the
key players of the
Bible.

...discover that
the Bible was
written for you.

There your Bible sits. Big, thick,
covered with dark cowhide—
and threatening. When you
approach it, you can almost hear
the theme from *Jaws* pounding
in your head.

Ever felt that way? You've
tried to read your copy of God's
Word. Maybe you've even used
one of those "read through the
Bible" programs (last year you made it all the way to mid-
February). But you just can't seem to stay interested. You know
you *should* read it. And you sincerely want to know God better. But it just feels so hard to relate to the Bible.

If you identify with these feelings, you're not alone.

Sometimes I pick up my Bible and God has something to say to me immediately. Other times I read a passage, scratch my head, and ask, "I wonder what that's all about?"

John Bunyan, the man who gave us *Pilgrim's Progress*, once admitted: "I have sometimes seen more in a line of the Bible than I could well tell how to stand under, and yet at another time the whole Bible hath been to me as dry as a stick."[1]

In this chapter, I want to help you relate to the Bible in ways that can turn resistance into anticipation.

CHOOSE YOUR BEST TRANSLATION

The Bible was originally written in three languages, and likely none is your mother tongue.

- Most of the Old Testament was written in Hebrew, the language of the Jewish people from the time of Abraham onward.
- A small portion of the Old Testament, composed after the Babylonian exile, was written in Aramaic because this had become the more common language of the people.[2] Aramaic was the language which Jesus most frequently spoke.
- The New Testament was written in Greek—not the classical Greek of Socrates and Homer, but *koine* Greek, the common Greek of the streets.

Many wonderful tools are available today that can help you understand the meaning of a Bible word even if you don't read the original languages.[3] But let's face it—the main language barrier for most of us is English.

When I was a boy, we only had one version of the Bible in our house, the King James. I memorized most of the Bible verses I know in King James. Even today, when I use a concordance, the word I want to find comes to my mind in KJV English. Growing up I had trouble with antiquated expressions like the "superfluity of naughtiness" (James 1:21, KJV) or "evil concupiscence" (Colossians 3:5, KJV). Who wouldn't? But by and large I understood what the translators were saying. Not everyone today, however, has had the same background I had. But fortunately we have many other contemporary translations available.

Don't fail to read the Bible simply because you have difficulty relating to the translation. Find a version you *do* understand. I'm often asked which version of the Bible I think is the best, and I always respond, "The one you read." It doesn't matter if you are convinced your version is the most accurate there is. If you don't read it, you won't connect with God.

Hurdle the language barrier by choosing a Bible that is comfortable for you. Then read it for all it's worth.

Find the Meanings in the Message

If you want your Bible to come alive, soak up the meaning of the most important words. How do you determine which words are most meaningful?

First, check out the verbs. Verbs are where the action is. Read the story of the prodigal son in Luke 15. Take note of the verbs in verse 20. When the young man was still far off, "his father *saw* him and *had compassion*, and *ran* and *fell* on his neck and *kissed* him" (NKJV). Those key verbs reveal worlds of truth about the father's love for the prodigal—and our Father's love for us.

Second, look at nouns, especially the power words—doctrinal words like redemption, salvation, forgiveness, and reconciliation and Christian living words like "love, joy, peace, patience, kindness, goodness, faithfulness, gentleness and self-control" (Galatians 5:22–23).

Third, take in the Bible's great word pictures. Who can resist the images of a shepherd rescuing one lost sheep, a prophet winging his way heavenward in a flaming chariot, or a Savior's body pierced by nails and hanging on a cross? Pictures like those can stay with you—and speak to your spirit—for your entire life.

Often the Bible uses picture words to describe God. David described God with a string of meaningful images in Psalm 18: "The LORD is my rock, my fortress and my deliverer; my God is my rock, in whom I take refuge. He is my shield and the horn of my salvation, my stronghold. I call to the LORD, who is worthy of praise, and I am saved from my enemies" (vv. 2–3).

LEARN THE LAY OF THE LAND

Did you know the cities of Caesarea and Philippi, when joined together, do *not* make Caesarea Philippi?

Caesarea was a magnificent harbor city on the Mediterranean coast of Israel, built by Herod the Great between today's Tel Aviv and Haifa. Here Paul was imprisoned for two years prior to being sent to Rome for trial before Caesar (Acts 24:27).

Philippi, on the other hand, was one of the chief cities of Macedonia in northern Greece. This Roman colony was where Lydia responded to the gospel, and Paul and Silas were imprisoned (Acts 16:14, 22–24), and the Philippian jailer was saved (vv. 29–31). The epistle of Philippians was written to the church in this Greek city.

But Caesarea Philippi was a town in the far north of Israel, near the foot of Mt. Hermon and the headwaters of the Jordan. This is where Jesus won that moving confession of faith from Peter: "You are the Christ, the Son of the living God" (Matthew 16:16).

Spending a couple of hours with a map of the biblical world can help you immensely in connecting with God. For one thing, you'll discover that Israel is oriented north and south, not east and west. The coastal plain rises gently and then more abruptly to the hill country of Ephraim and Judah. Then it suddenly and precipitously drops down into the great rift valley, including the Dead Sea, the lowest spot on earth. After you cross the Jordan Valley the land begins to rise again to the Transjordan Plateau, including the hills of Gilead, Ammon, and Moab.

Since traveling north or south over the mountainous terrain of central Israel was difficult, when Jesus journeyed from Galilee to Jerusalem and back, He would descend into the Jordan Valley, cross the river, and use the valley highway. This made the urgency of His journey through Samaria in John 4 more of a divine appointment than a geographical necessity. Understanding the lay of the land helps you relate to that.

Also, have you noticed that whenever people in the Bible traveled to Jerusalem, they always talked about going "up to

Jerusalem"? In fact, Psalms 120–134 are designated as "Songs of Ascents" and were sung by pilgrims ascending the roads to Jerusalem. That's because Jerusalem is situated on the high hills of Judea.

A personal journey to the Holy Land is a much better teacher, of course, but even a little understanding of Bible geography will flash new insights from God's Word to you and help you connect with Him.

STAND BACK FROM THE TREES (AND LOOK AT THE FOREST)

Of all the strange and eerie phenomena on our planet (the stone ring at Stonehenge, the expressionless statues of Easter Island, etc.), none is stranger than the lines on the Nazca Plains of Peru. For years, historians, archaeologists, and just plain folks were mystified by these intriguing lines.

In 1939, Dr. Paul Kosok of Long Island University discovered that their true meaning could be understood only from the air. A couple of years ago I flew with a Peruvian pilot over the Nazca Plain. From our vantage point, it was evident these strange lines were strings of rocks that formed enormous drawings of birds, insects, animals, and other creatures. From a distance the artwork became clear.

Sometimes in order to connect with God, you just have to stand back from the trees (words, phrases, and individual stories) and look at the forest (the bigger picture of who God is and how He is at work in our world).

Take the most important example: *The life of Jesus would*

appear to be a tragic waste if you saw it as lasting only thirty-three years and ending at the cross. But if you step back and see how His life fits into the sovereign plan of God, the tragedy disappears.

Here's the big picture of the life of Jesus:

- Before time began, God's plan of salvation through Jesus' life, death, and resurrection was charted by the Trinity (Ephesians 1:4–5).
- All through the Old Testament years, there were hints of the coming Savior (Isaiah 7:14; 9:6; 11:1, 10; Jeremiah 23:5; Micah 5:2).
- Then, "when the time had fully come, God sent his Son, born of a woman, born under law, to redeem those under law, that we might receive the full rights of sons" (Galatians 4:4–5).
- Jesus' life did not end at Calvary. Three days later He rose from the dead, defeating death forever. Forty days later (Acts 1:3), He ascended into heaven (Acts 1:11), where He awaits the day He will come again to catch us up with Him (1 Thessalonians 4:13–18).
- One day Jesus will return to earth in power and great glory (Matthew 24:30) as King of kings and Lord of lords (Revelation 19:16), when "the kingdom of the world has become the kingdom of our Lord and of his Christ, and he will reign for ever and ever" (11:15).

So go ahead and examine the trees close up, but be ready, too, to stand back and take in the grand panorama of God's work.

ENJOY THE VARIETY

The reason the Bible does not disappoint readers with many interests is that the book itself features many literary forms. The Bible has something for everyone:

- Adventures—David and Goliath; Daniel in the lions' den; Paul's shipwreck.
- Love stories—Abraham and Sarah; Boaz and Ruth; Joseph and Mary.
- Loyal friendships: Joshua and Caleb; David and Jonathan; Paul and Timothy.
- Intimate letters—Paul writing to Timothy and Philemon.
- Convincing arguments—the books of Romans and Hebrews, for example.
- Compelling history—the books of Samuel and Kings, for example, and the book of Acts.
- Close-up biography—the four Gospels.
- Collected wise sayings—Proverbs and James.
- Devotional poetry—the book of Psalms.
- Prophecies of what is to come—Isaiah, for example, or Revelation.

And that's just a quick overview.

To relate to the Bible best, make sure you understand what kind of literature you're reading. That will help you know what to look for and how to read it. If you're not sure, a study Bible or commentary can help.

GET TO KNOW THE MAIN CHARACTERS

Okay, let's play a game. I'll give you the names of the most important characters, and you tell me where to find them. Bustopher Jones, Mungojerrie and Rumpelteazer, Mr. Mistoffelees, Grizabella, and Old Deuteronomy. Of course, you'll find them in the long-running Broadway production of *Cats*, based on poetry by T. S. Elliot. How about this one? Claudius, Gertrude, Polonius, Rosencrantz, Guildenstern, and Ophelia. A little harder, maybe? They're from Shakespeare's *Hamlet*. Let's try a movie. There's Mayor Shinn, Tommy, Winthrop, Marion the Librarian, and Professor Harold Hill. That's the classic movie *The Music Man*.

Most of us can quickly identify with those characters. We know their quirks and foibles, as well as what made them loved (or not).

If you want to connect with God, get to know the key players in His Word. You'll want to know the great patriarchs of the Jewish people—Abraham, Isaac, Jacob, and Joseph. You'll want to become familiar with the life stories of heroes like Samuel, Elijah, Isaiah, Stephen, and Paul. You'll want to walk with the twelve disciples as they follow Jesus.

But more than anyone else, find the Son of God—the central Person in all of Scripture. Only Jesus is called the "Lamb of God who takes away the sin of the world" (John 1:29). Only Jesus left behind the glory of heaven to be born in a Bethlehem stable (Luke 2). Only Jesus taught as never a man had taught before and lived what He taught (Matthew 5). (We'll come back to the importance of Jesus' life in chapter 12.)

If you get to know His story, and some of the other main characters in Scripture, you'll find it much easier to relate to God's Word and understand His heart.

PART TWO

Why the Bible Can
Change Your Live

Now that you're ready to connect with God through the Bible, what should you expect? What will you discover? How will you change?

Part 2 of this book focuses on benefits. We'll look at how your relationship with God will undergo a radical transformation, how your understanding of yourself will change, and how your daily life will shift—from confusion and meaninglessness to clarity centeredness, and overflowing hope.

5

THROUGH THE BIBLE, YOU GET TO KNOW GOD

What a vast distance there is between knowing God and loving Him.

—BLAISE PASCAL

IN THIS CHAPTER...

...learn what it means to get to know God.

...discover the ways you get to know God.

...identify what you can know intimately about God.

Recently, the *BBC News World Edition* reported that a growing group of *Star Wars* fans have become adherents to the "Jedi religion." In Australia alone, more than seventy thousand people describe themselves as Jedi who believe they get power from "the force," a mysterious energy field first imagined in the Star Wars films. In the United Kingdom, "Jedi Knight" is now included by census authorities on the list of religions.[1]

Is God simply a "force" in your life—kind and good, but unknowable and impersonal? Or is He a personal friend?

How you answer will determine what you expect from your spiritual life.

The force question, as trendy as it seems, predates George Lucas films by several millennia. One of Job's friends, Zophar the Naamathite, wondered, "Can you fathom the mysteries of God? Can you probe the limits of the Almighty? They are higher than the heavens—what can you do?" (Job 11:7–8). The fifteenth-century German philosopher and theologian Nicholas of Cusa once mused about God: "Thou canst not be known, unless the unknowable could be known, and the invisible beheld, and the inaccessible attained."[2]

Intimacy with that kind of God certainly sounds challenging, doesn't it? But while He cannot be known *completely*, God can be known *personally* and *truly*. And furthermore, that is how He *wants* to be known. That's the wonderful promise of the gospel—and the life-changing opportunity we have whenever we open our Bibles.

Let's look further.

WHAT THE BIBLE SHOWS US ABOUT GOD

The good news of the Bible is that both God's character and His record with people like you and me make knowing Him the discovery of a lifetime. Here are truths about Him every human being can know for certain—truths that can change your life and mine, starting today:

God is alive.

Thirty times in the Bible He is referred to as "the living God." Jeremiah proclaimed, "But the LORD is the true God; he is the living God, the eternal King" (10:10). When Jesus asked Peter who He was, Peter affirmed, "You are the Christ, the Son of the living God" (Matthew 16:16). It was his intense desire to become intimate with God that drove the psalmist to declare, "My soul thirsts for God, for the living God" (Psalm 42:2). If God were not alive, our efforts to connect with Him would fail. If He were not alive, our desire to connect with Him would vanish. "My soul longs, yes, even faints for the courts of the LORD; my heart and my flesh cry out for the living God" (Psalm 84:2, NKJV). That cry would fall on deaf ears if God weren't alive.

God is personal.

You have to be impressed with how often the possessive personal pronoun *my* is used when the Bible writers speak of God. He is not a belief system or an unknowable force. He is God up close and personal. Even in the Old Testament— before He came to earth as a person—the personal pronoun *my* is coupled with *God* 130 times.

> The LORD is my rock, my fortress and my deliverer; my God is my rock, in whom I take refuge. He is my shield and the horn of my salvation, my stronghold. I call to the LORD, who is worthy of praise, and I am saved from my enemies. (Psalm 18:2–3)

That's personal.

God is near.

True, writers of the Bible often depicted God as high and exalted (Isaiah 6:1), His throne surrounded by worshipping angels, seraphs, and elders (Revelation 4–5). But God has also made Himself accessible to everyone. As Oliver Wendell Holmes wrote:

> Lord of all being, throned afar,
>   Thy glory flames from sun and star;
> Center and soul of every sphere,
>   Yet to each loving heart how near!

The Bible often speaks of how near God is to us. "You are near, O LORD," writes the psalmist (119:151), and, "The LORD is close to the brokenhearted" (34:18), and, "The LORD is near to all who call on him, to all who call on him in truth" (145:18). Isaiah begs his people, "Seek the LORD while he may be found; call on him while he is near" (55:6).

God is moral.

You can gaze at the stars and sense God's power, but to know if you can trust His character, you have to read His Word. The Bible tells us that God is both morally pure and perfect. For example: "Your eyes are too pure to look on evil; you cannot tolerate wrong" (Habakkuk 1:13), and, "Holy, holy, holy is the LORD Almighty" (Isaiah 6:3).

Because God is holy—and *only* God is holy—He is the standard for what is moral and ethical. In other words, right is right if God does it. And the redemptive promise of the

Gospel is that as we become intimate with the God who is both moral and ethical, His Spirit will continually be at work in us to change our nature to become more like His.

God is good.

Even though our world has been ruined by sin, there is still a great deal of evidence for God's goodness all around. David wrote:

> Praise the LORD, O my soul, and forget not all his benefits—who forgives all your sins and heals all your diseases, who redeems your life from the pit and crowns you with love and compassion, who satisfies your desires with good things so that your youth is renewed like the eagle's. (Psalm 103:2–5)

It's easy to believe in the goodness of God when you are sick and He heals you. The Bible reveals that God also forgives all your sins and redeems your life. And even more—no matter what evil happens in this world, the God of this world is still only good!

God loves you more than anybody does.

So deep is God's love for you that He not only declared it in the Bible; He demonstrated it. Paul put it this way:

> Very rarely will anyone die for a righteous man, though for a good man someone might possibly dare to die. But God demonstrates his own love for us in

this: While we were still sinners, Christ died for us. (Romans 5:7–8)

The best-known verse in the Bible says:

"For God so loved the world that he gave his one and only Son, that whoever believes in him shall not perish but have eternal life. For God did not send his Son into the world to condemn the world, but to save the world through him." (John 3:16–17)

And if you've already responded to God's love, there's even better news. You can never be detached from God's love. Paul wrote:

For I am convinced that neither death nor life, neither angels nor demons, neither the present nor the future, nor any powers, neither height nor depth, nor anything else in all creation, will be able to separate us from the love of God that is in Christ Jesus our Lord. (Romans 8:38–39)

God gives people a second chance.

We all need a second chance now and then. Maybe you've given in to some sin that you aren't proud of. Confess that sin for what it is, repent of it, and God will forgive you (1 John 1:9). Will God pick you up and give you a second chance in life? The Bible says yes—and shows that He's eager to do so.

Jonah was a wrong-way prophet. Called to go to Nineveh,

he sailed the other way instead. But God got his attention with a great wind and a violent storm. God saved Jonah's life by providing safe haven in a large fish. In the belly of the fish, Jonah repented of his rebellion. And God gave Jonah a second chance—"Then the word of the LORD came to Jonah a second time" (Jonah 3:1).

After boasting that he would never forsake the Lord, Peter did exactly that three times (Matthew 26:69–75). But Jesus personally and gently led Peter through his steps of repentance. He asked a simple question: "Do you love me?" (John 21:15–17). Later Peter became the principal preacher of Christianity in the first century. When you get to know Him intimately, you'll discover (and treasure) what so many before you have—that God is a God of second chances.

God provides eternal life.

Jesus prayed to His Father the night before His crucifixion and said:

> "Father, the time has come. Glorify your Son, that your Son may glorify you. For you granted him authority over all people that he might give eternal life to all those you have given him. Now this is eternal life: that they may know you, the only true God, and Jesus Christ, whom you have sent." (John 17:1–3)

God not only provides eternal life through His Son; by definition, to know God personally and truly is to have eternal life.

We've talked about who God is, but maybe we should

focus on those things that cause us to miss our goal of know-ing Him intimately. As you'll see, it's nearly always a case of good that is robbing us of the best thing.

WHAT CAN KEEP YOU
FROM KNOWING GOD

Jim Elliot. Nate Saint. Roger Youderian. Ed McCully. Pete Fleming. Five brave missionaries martyred by the Auca Indians in 1956. Their names are burned into the book of God's heroes, and their lives inspired a generation to dedicate them-selves to spreading the Gospel.

One entry in Jim Elliot's personal journal is especially meaningful for this chapter. He wrote:

> Oh, the fullness, pleasure, sheer excitement of know-ing God on Earth! I care not if I never raise my voice again for Him, if only I may love Him, please Him. Perhaps in mercy He shall give me a host of children that I may lead them through the vast star fields to explore His delicacies whose finger ends set them to burning. But if not, if only I may see Him, touch His garments, smile into His eyes—ah then, not stars nor children shall matter, only Himself.[3]

In his relationship with God, Elliot longed for much more than familiarity with an idea or set of beliefs. He desperately wanted a personal connection—and that kind of relationship gave his life incredible power and joy.

Paul expressed the same kind of desire when he wrote, "I

want to know Christ" (Philippians 3:10). I don't think he meant he wanted to learn *about* Jesus Christ. Like David, Paul physically, spiritually, and emotionally longed for God (Psalm 63:1). That's evident from his reference to the Lord's suffering: "I want to know Christ and the power of his resurrection and the fellowship of sharing in his sufferings, becoming like him in his death" (Philippians 3:10).

Even if you spend time seeking God in His Word, what might keep you from the depth of intimacy that the heroes of the faith experienced? Three common misunderstandings that keep many from genuinely knowing God:

1. Knowing God and knowledge of God are not the same.

Theology students study God, but not all become intimate with Him. In fact, I've met busy farmers with holes in the knees of their jeans who know God better than some theologians. To know God intimately is to take what you learn of Him from His Word and to use it as the path to His heart.

Knowledge, you see, is a means to an end: God Himself is the end. People who only get the knowledge of God without becoming intimate with Him become what the term *sophomore* implies: a wise fool.

2. Knowing God and knowing how to know God are not the same.

You've met them and so have I—people who have mastered the Romans Road, the Four Spiritual Laws, Evangelism Explosion, and every other means of presenting the gospel.

They have talked to hundreds of people about their need for a Savior. They know how to know God and are willing to share this with anyone at any time. But they are so burdened for the lost that they don't take time to become intimate with the God they want to share.

On resurrection morning, before Jesus told the women to "go quickly and tell," He commanded them to "come and see" (Matthew 28:6–7). Until we have spent some intimate time with the Savior, we will be an inadequate ambassador for Him. Before we can "go and tell" we must "come and see."

3. Knowing God and experiencing God are not the same.

In some circles today, Christians have wrongly equated knowing God with a euphoric or moving emotional experience. They have confused ecstasy with intimacy. There were believers like that in the Corinthian church too. Paul said they were only looking on the surface of things (2 Corinthians 10:7). He claimed, "We demolish arguments and every pretension that sets itself up against the knowledge of God" (v. 5).

Knowing God intimately is always accompanied by behavioral change. Paul knew that the Roman believers had connected with God through His Word because they were "full of goodness, complete in knowledge and competent to instruct one another" (Romans 15:14). Truly knowing God manifests itself in love (1 Corinthians 13:2), spreads a godly fragrance (2 Corinthians 2:14), and is coupled with purity, patience, and kindness (6:6). It teams up with grace (Ephesians 1:7–8), unity, and maturity (4:13). It gives depth of insight (Philippians 1:9), a worthy life, and much fruit (Colossians 1:10).

So don't settle for picking up a little knowledge of God through your study group. Don't be cheated by knowing how to know God. Sit down with your Bible, and ask God to give you that deep desire that David and Paul had. Ask Him to take your present knowledge and lead you forward into intimacy with Him.

6

THROUGH THE BIBLE, YOU DISCOVER WHO YOU ARE

The destined end of man is not happiness,
nor health, but holiness.

—OSWALD CHAMBERS

IN THIS CHAPTER...

...learn that you were created by God with great significance.

...uncover how you lost that significance.

...discover your new significance in Christ.

If you've ever watched the Academy Awards, the Country Music Awards, or any other television special to honor people, you know that we tend to be wrapped up in our achievements. Most people gain their significance from who they are or what they can do that is worthy of recognition.

How you view yourself and others—and how you then order your life—is sometimes called a paradigm. The Bible says that, over time, the paradigm by which people live their lives has changed.

FIRST CAME THE
"CREATED-SIGNIFICANT" PARADIGM

The Bible says that you are a significant person because you were created that way. Human life began under the "created-significant" paradigm. The first book of the Bible describes just how significant our first parents were to God. Here's what the Bible says makes you significant.

The order of your creation

God's creation began with basic elements. He created water, sunlight, vegetation, and animals all in a necessary sequence. God did not create plant life before creating the sun because plants need sunlight for photosynthesis. There was order to God's creation.

But nowhere is that order more evident than when God came to the crown of His creation—mankind. "Then God said, 'Let us make man in our image'" (Genesis 1:26). He saved the best until last. You are the crown of God's creation, the final capstone.

The method of creation

For everything else God made, He simply spoke and things came to be. The writer of Hebrews indicates the "universe was formed at God's command" (11:3) and that He continues "sustaining all things by his powerful word" (1:3). When God spoke, things appeared.

But that was not true for *Homo sapiens*. God didn't just

speak Adam into existence. Instead, "The LORD God formed the man from the dust of the ground" (Genesis 2:7). God took common dirt, the elements of the earth, and formed the first man as a potter would manually shape an exquisite vase. Nothing else in God's creation can claim this exception to the rule, but you can.[1]

The breath of creation

Genesis 2:7 continues, "The Lord God formed the man from the dust of the ground and breathed into his nostrils the breath of life, and the man became a living being." Becoming a living being is not the uniqueness here; that same Hebrew phrase is used of both sea and land animals (1:20–21, 24). What is unique is that God breathed from His mouth directly into Adam's nostrils. Adam's first breath came directly from God.

The breath of God in us makes us conscious of our relationship with God. It's that relationship that gives us significance.

Interestingly, the Bible records only one other occasion when the Almighty breathed out of His mouth:

> All Scripture is God-breathed and is useful for teaching, rebuking, correcting and training in righteousness, so that the man of God may be thoroughly equipped for every good work. (2 Timothy 3:16–17)

God breathed into you, giving you a special relationship with Him; He breathed into His Word, giving it a special relationship with Him.

The image of creation

Other living things were created "according to their kinds" (see Genesis 1:11–12, 21, 24–25). But immediately after the final use of that phrase, God says, "Let us make man *in our image, in our likeness*" (v. 26). This expression is invested with a special solemnity.[2]

To be created in the image of God means that we share, however imperfectly, in the nature of God. Unlike the animals, we are articulate communicators; we are aware of the relationship between ourselves, eternity, and God; and we are capable of wisely pursuing justice and holiness because we have an innate discernment of right and wrong.

The similarity in creation

But we were created in God's likeness as well as in His image. This expression implies being similar but not an exact duplicate. Genesis 5:1 repeats, "When God created man, he made him in the likeness of God." The word *likeness*[3] here means we resemble God in certain ways. For example, God is a Trinity (Father, Son, and Holy Spirit); we humans are tripartite creatures consisting of spirit, soul, and body. Animals are body and soul, but they have no spiritual consciousness of God.

We were created by God as the most significant part of His creation. When life began, human beings were blessed to live under the "created-significant" paradigm. But then something terrible happened....

Then Came the "Significance-Lost" Paradigm

In the Garden of Eden, Adam and Eve were totally dependent upon God, and that was okay because that connection gave them significance. But when Adam and Eve sinned, they renounced the "created-significant" paradigm. They chose independence from God over relationship with Him.

As you would expect, every man and woman since then has struggled with confusion about identity and feelings of insignificance. Many people go through life identifying with the famous line from Shakespeare's *Macbeth*: "[Life] is a tale told by an idiot, full of sound and fury, signifying nothing."[4]

Because feelings of insignificance are universal to humans, we all try in different ways to regain significance. Some turn to physical accomplishments. Others turn to the pursuit of money, status, creative accomplishment, power, pleasure, or fame.

But while these sometimes lead to fulfillment, they do not lead to significance.

King Solomon was like that. He had all the trappings of success and significance. He was both fabulously wealthy and exceptionally brilliant. When the queen of Sheba came to see if the tales about Solomon were true (2 Chronicles 9:1), she gasped, "Indeed, not even half the greatness of your wisdom was told me" (v. 6).

Solomon had everything, but you'd never know it. Read what he wrote:

> I said to myself, "Have fun and enjoy yourself!" But this didn't make sense. Laughing and having fun is

crazy. What good does it do? I wanted to find out what was best for us during the short time we have on this earth. So I decided to make myself happy with wine and find out what it means to be foolish, without really being foolish myself. I did some great things. I built houses and planted vineyards. I got whatever I wanted and did whatever made me happy. But most of all, I enjoyed my work. Then I thought about everything I had done, including the hard work, and it was simply chasing the wind. Nothing on earth is worth the trouble. This made me hate life. Everything we do is painful: it's just as senseless as chasing the wind. (Ecclesiastes 2:1–4, 10–11, 17, CEV)

I believe that the search for significance is the most significant search of mankind. But if our significance is found in insignificant things, our search itself becomes insignificant.

Fortunately, Christ came to return what humanity had lost.

NOW WE HAVE THE "SIGNIFICANCE-RECOVERED" PARADIGM

You see, what you lost when your dependent relationship with God was severed by sin can only be restored when that relationship is dependent again. That's exactly what Jesus Christ did at Calvary's cross. He sacrificed Himself for you and met all the requirements of God to pay for your sin. And when you trust Him alone and what He did as your Savior, you again admit your dependence on God, which restores your significance.

You begin to live under the significance-recovered paradigm. You are a brand-new creation in Christ Jesus (2 Corinthians 5:17). You are not just a refurbished loser; you have become a redeemed winner.

Once you become a Christian, you begin to live under a new paradigm, and you need to begin looking at yourself differently, more realistically, more positively, more biblically. Here's what the Bible says about who you *really* are once you have reconnected with God through faith in Christ Jesus.

You are God's own handiwork.

If someone told you that you were "a real piece of work," you wouldn't necessarily feel complimented. But Ephesians 2:10 tells every believer in Christ, "For we are God's workmanship, created in Christ Jesus to do good works, which God prepared in advance for us to do." You are again the work of God's hands, being recreated with significance.

You are a saint.

Though some have come to believe that a saint is someone who has died and is now beatified, the Bible presents an entirely different reality. If you have a right relationship with God through faith in Christ as Savior, you *are* a saint. This is why Paul wrote letters to the "saints" in Rome (Romans 1:7), Ephesus (Ephesians 1:1), Colosse (Colossians 1:2, NKJV), Corinth (1 Corinthians 1:2, NKJV), and Philippi (Philippians 1:1). He was writing to ordinary believers—people who had been saved from sin and now wanted to live a righteous life.

When you read your Bible, you too will discover how to become a saint. If you are born again, feel free to call yourself a saint—but act like one too. That's what "significant" people do.

You are God's own child.

For most of us, no word evokes more pleasant memories than *family*. We love being a part of ours, or we deeply long to create one that fulfills the promise of that word. In Christ Jesus, you are a part of God's family. John caught the wonder of it when he exclaimed, "How great is the love the Father has lavished on us, that we should be called children of God! And that is what we are!" (1 John 3:1).

To belong to God's family means you enjoy all the rights and privileges of being related to God. You have a name, Christian (Acts 11:26), and that identifies you with Jesus Christ your brother (Hebrews 2:11). You have a blood relationship, redeemed with the precious blood of Christ (1 Peter 1:18–19). You have a lawful standing, legally adopted as God's child (Romans 8:15–16). You have a place to belong, a place to call home, a family to call your own.

You are living with recovered significance as part of God's family.

You are God's heir.

One day my elderly mother was fretting about how much medical costs were cutting into their nest egg. "Dad and I aren't going to have anything to leave to you," she told us.

After assuring her that her concern should not be for us, but for my father and herself, I said, "Besides, I have two fathers, both of whom I love dearly. One lives on earth and is broke; the other lives in heaven and is fabulously wealthy."

When we trust Christ as our Savior, "we are heirs—heirs of God and co-heirs with Christ" (Romans 8:17). Everything that belongs to our heavenly Father belongs to His Son and heir, Jesus Christ; and everything that belongs to Jesus belongs to His coheirs, you and me. Being God's heir includes proximity to the Father, an exceptional place of service in His Kingdom, family identification with the Sovereign Lord, access to God's throne, and so much more that money can't buy. It is a connection with the greatest significance possible.

You are a special person.

Most people long to be special. But what really makes being special wonderful is the person who thinks we're special. If a person you hardly knew said, "Thank you. You're special," you might not get overly excited. But if the president of the United States told you the same thing, you'd probably remember it for the rest of your life.

When you live by the significance-recovered paradigm, it is God who thinks you're special. "But you are a chosen people, a royal priesthood, a holy nation, a people belonging to God" (1 Peter 2:9). "A people specifically belonging to God" was initially used as a designation for God's chosen people, Israel (Exodus 19:5; Deuteronomy 14:2; 26:18; Psalm 135:4), but both Paul (Titus 2:14) and Peter (1 Peter 2:9) used it of God's people chosen for salvation. It means you belong to God, you are bought with the price of His Son's blood (1 Corinthians 6:19–20), and you now follow the blood-stained banner of Prince Emmanuel and enjoy the privileges of being special to God.

You are an ambassador for Christ.

I once sat on an airplane next to an obviously successful business-man. He was quick to tell me so. When he asked what I did for a living, I hesitated. A menu of options ran through my mind. I could say that I was the president and CEO of a multimillion-dollar, multinational corporation; surely that would impress him. I could say that I was an author; he probably had never written a book. I could say that I was a radio personality; there wouldn't have been many of those on the plane.

Finally, I went another route. I said, "I'm an ambassador." That got his attention.

But I *am* an ambassador, and so are you! When you place your faith in Jesus Christ as Savior, you become an ambassa-dor for Christ (2 Corinthians 5:20). An ambassador is one who officially represents another. As an ambassador for Christ, your significance doesn't come in who you are; it comes in whom you represent. You represent the King of kings and Lord of lords.

NO ONE CAN TAKE IT FROM YOU

Even on your most difficult days, who you are in Christ is cer-tain, final, and theft-proof! Your identity is assured—even on those days when you feel like young Eric Greene…

All Eric wanted to do was enjoy his vacation, but things turned out very differently. After a morning transaction at a local bank in the Harrisburg, Pennsylvania, area, Eric returned home to enjoy his time off. Later that day the police kicked in his door and pointed their guns at him. Then they arrested him and charged him with stealing sixty thousand dollars from the bank in an armed robbery that very morning.

"I didn't understand why they had arrested me," said the twenty-six-year-old Greene. "I kept trying to tell myself, 'I'm on vacation.'"

Later, the police chief admitted it had been a case of mistaken identity. An eighteen-year-old was eventually arrested and charged with the crime. Eric Greene wasn't a bank robber after all.

So who are you…really? One person among billions? An aging body made up of biodegradable chemicals? A sin-tainted being?

Yes, all of those things. But when you read your Bible, you discover that you are much more. You are God's heir, His own handiwork, a saint, an ambassador. This is not simple self-esteem; this is the transformation that takes place in a life that has come to grips with the claims of God's Word and believed them. This is living under the significance-recovered paradigm.

This is who you are in Christ Jesus…and no one on earth can take it away.

7 THROUGH THE BIBLE, YOU FIND YOUR CENTER

*When you read God's Word, you must constantly
be saying to yourself, "It is talking to me, and about me."*
—SØREN KIERKEGAARD

IN THIS CHAPTER...

...learn how to use the Bible to find the "center" of your personal life.

...discover personal fulfillment through the Bible.

...make the Bible the center of your family life.

I grew up in the tiny town of Fombell, about fifty miles north of Pittsburgh, Pennsylvania. My hometown was so small that it had only one commercial building, which housed the post office, general store, train station, and gas station. I remember my father buying candy for me at that store—a penny a piece. That old building is gone now, but every few years I return to where it stood. It's good to go back to the old places, to remember who you are, to return to the center of your existence.

What would you say is the "center" of your spiritual pilgrimage? What is the True North on your spiritual compass? I hope you're seeing that the Bible is the "center" you've been looking for in your life.

That's what this chapter is all about.

THE BIBLE IS THE CENTER OF YOUR SPIRITUAL STABILITY

Do you ever feel like you are on a spiritual roller coaster, up one day and down the next? Most of us have felt that way at one time. But, we don't have to live as victims of feelings and circumstances. While we are created as complex and emotional beings, the Bible shows how to purposefully increase in stability and maturity as we grow in Christ.

Here's one example of what I mean: In Colossians 1:9–10, Paul shows how the Bible can function as the center of our spiritual journey (notice especially the italicized words):

> For this reason, since the day we heard about you, we have not stopped praying for you and asking God to fill you with the *knowledge* of his will through all *spiritual wisdom* and *understanding*. And we pray this in order that you may live *a life worthy* of the Lord and may please him in every way: *bearing fruit* in every *good work*, growing in the knowledge of God.

Now, rather than see your spiritual growth as a series of hills and valleys, picture it as the face on a clock:

1. KNOWLEDGE. When you use the Bible to discover the center to your spiritual growth, you begin at twelve o'clock by filling yourself with the knowledge of God's will (Colossians 1:9). How do you do that? Read God's Word. Not only are there many places in the Bible that specifically say "this is the will of God for you," but passage after passage direct you to know what God wants for you and from you.[1] The road of steady growth toward spiritual maturity begins when you become acquainted with what's written in the Bible.

2. SPIRITUAL WISDOM. Your general knowledge of what's included in the Bible is only your starting point. Move to two o'clock on your clock, and add to your knowledge the wisdom that only comes from God (v. 9). This is the spiritual shrewdness that comes when you meditate on His Word, allowing it to "marinate" your life in His wisdom. This kind of wisdom displays deeper insights than

can be gained by reading alone. It takes time, but it's worth it because it moves you further along on the cycle of spiritual growth.

3. UNDERSTANDING. Now go to four o'clock, and add a deep understanding of the Word. You accomplish this when you bring together in one worldview all you've read, comparing Scripture with Scripture, and begin to mold a framework on which to hang all of God's truth. Understanding is what Jesus showed at age twelve when He astonished everyone in the temple (Luke 2:47). They couldn't believe that someone so young could draw from so many parts of God's Word and make sense of the whole. That's genuine understanding. It probably won't come the first time you read something. But ask the Holy Spirit to teach you, and He will take you to a new level of spiritual insight.

4. WORTHY LIFE. If you stopped there, you might have a handle on God's Word, but you wouldn't make much of an impact on the world. So move on to six o'clock. Here, the cycle of spiritual growth has moved from observation to application. Now the truths of the Word can have great power in your life to draw you closer to God and let Him change your values and attitudes (Psalm 119:9, 105, 133). Now you can know that when you walk according to what you read in God's Word, you walk according to God's will.

5. BEAR FRUIT. You're now at eight o'clock. You want to bear fruit for the One who loves you and gave Himself for you. Colossians 1:10 demonstrates that the Bible is the center for your personal spirituality by instructing and encourag-

ing you to become a fruit-bearing disciple. After all, that's what Jesus said He wants from you (John 15:5, 8). And when your life is spiritually vibrant, others will notice.

6. GOOD WORK. Move on to ten o'clock. Bearing fruit also means that you work for the Lord, doing whatever He asks of you, whenever and wherever He asks it. In fact, it is in "every good work" that your fruit is demonstrated. Don't spend your life on things that perish, but invest it in things that endure throughout eternity (John 6:27). Whatever God calls you to do for Him, do it with all your might (Ecclesiastes 9:10), because spiritual work is always eternal work.

7. BACK TO KNOWLEDGE. Now you're back to twelve o'clock, right where you started, and you're ready to delve deeper into the knowledge of God and His Word. As you do, your cycle of spiritual growth will begin all over again, taking you closer and closer to the kind of life and intimacy with God that He desires for you.

When you center your personal spirituality in the Bible, you minimize the ups and downs in life and enjoy the ride much more! You won't find that formula for spiritual stability in any other books—only in *the* Book.

THE BIBLE IS YOUR CENTER FOR YOUR PERSONAL AWARENESS OF GOD

I remember seeing a young man sitting cross-legged in front of what he considered a sacred stone in Macchu Picchu, the ancient city of the Incas high in the Andes of Peru. He was in a trance, seeking personal awareness of God.

Everywhere people are struggling to discover God, but they are failing to look for Him where He revealed Himself—in the pages of His Word.

Personal awareness of God comes through the person of God the Son, Jesus Christ. The Savior said to His disciples, "Anyone who has seen me has seen the Father" (John 14:9). When you read about Jesus in the Bible, you discover God. Paul helps us understand that in Colossians 1, where he gives fourteen reasons why we should exalt Jesus as God and Lord:

FOURTEEN REASONS TO EXALT THE LORD JESUS CHRIST

1. Jesus delivered us from the power of darkness (v. 13).
2. Jesus conveyed us into the kingdom of the Son (v. 13).
3. Jesus shed His blood for our redemption (v. 14).
4. Jesus is our Only Hope for forgiveness (v. 14).
5. Jesus is the Image of the invisible God (v. 15).[2]
6. Jesus is the Firstborn over all creation (v. 15).[3]
7. Jesus is the Creator of all things (v. 16).[4]
8. Jesus is the Sustainer of all He created (v. 17).
9. Jesus is the Head of the church (v. 18).[5]
10. Jesus is Firstborn from the dead (v. 18).[6]
11. Jesus is the Preeminent Person of history (v. 18).
12. Jesus is the Fullness of God (v. 19).[7]
13. Jesus is the Reconciler of things on earth and heaven to God (v. 20).
14. Jesus is our Peace Treaty with God (v. 20).[8]

Is it possible today for you to really know Jesus, a person who lived two millennia ago? And through Him, can you become personally aware of God?

The answer is: Yes, you can.

The Bible doesn't tell the story of Jesus as just a person caught in history, but as the full expression of God in human form—the focal point and culmination of the Bible story. And each of us is invited to a personal relationship with God through faith in Jesus as our Savior (Acts 16:31).

THE BIBLE IS YOUR CENTER FOR PERSONAL FULFILLMENT

Everybody wants to be fulfilled. I'm sure Lance Armstrong felt fulfillment as he won the Tour de France race after race. And Michael Jordan must have felt considerable personal gratification during his years of dominating the National Basketball Association. But personal fulfillment from any kind of event or achievement only applies to one aspect of our lives. It's partial and temporary, not total.

Listen to what Paul told the Colossians: "For in Christ all the *fullness* of the Deity lives in bodily form, and *you have been given fullness in Christ*, who is the head over every power and authority" (2:9–10). The life you and I can enjoy in Christ is characterized by "fullness."

I remember hearing a story of fulfillment in Christ from a man named Christian DiSanto. He was married to Paula and they had three sons, but Christian felt incomplete, searching for something. But he didn't know what. Paula went to church, but Christian was not interested in spiritual things.

Still, Paula was faithful and planted seeds of faith in her husband's life.

Then one day, when Christian was driving home from work, it happened. "I was listening to heavy metal music, and I found myself flipping through the dial, hitting the search button," he wrote in a letter. He wasn't looking for anybody like me, but when the radio stopped scanning, my voice was what Christian heard.

"I had never listened to *Back to the Bible* before," he said, "but you were talking about people's need for a Savior, to find the center in their lives. I knew a little bit about who Jesus was, but I wasn't living for Him. At that point I knew I was going to hell and there was nothing I could do to save myself other than to receive Jesus Christ as my Lord and Savior."

That is what Christian decided to do. A profound change came over his life. For the first time ever he felt personally fulfilled and at peace with God. "I came home and told Paula, and, boy, it was an amazing time. I could see the joy that came over her face. Everything's been different since then. It's just amazing."

If personal fulfillment is what you're searching for today, look no further than your Bible. When the Bible is the center for your life, personal fulfillment is the by-product.

THE BIBLE IS YOUR CENTER FOR
PERSONAL VALUES

Do you know the difference between values and virtues? Not many today do. No one has done more critical thinking in our time about the difference between values and virtues than

Gertrude Himmelfarb, professor emerita of history at University City College in New York City. In her classic, *The DeMoralization of Society*, Dr. Himmelfarb wrote:

> So long as morality was couched in the language of "virtue," it had a firm, resolute character. The older philosophers might argue about the source of virtues, the kinds and relative importance of virtues, the relation between moral and intellectual virtues or classical and religious ones or the bearing of private virtues upon public ones.... But for a particular people at a particular time, the word "virtue" carried with it a sense of gravity and authority, as "values" does not.[9]

Virtues are objective—they exist whether they are agreed upon, acknowledged, or lived by. Values, on the other hand, are subjective—everyone gets to pick their own. Virtues conform to a standard of right; values conform to the individual. But consider this: When you discover the virtues that are part of God's moral code, you discover the basis for values that please God, nourish you, and are a benefit to others.

So if you want to think like everybody else, read *USA Today*. If you want to think like God, read the Bible. Values that transcend everyday thinking usually have to come from outside everyday thinking. That's why Paul counsels us to "set your hearts on things above, where Christ is seated at the right hand of God. Set your minds on things above, not on earthly things" (Colossians 3:1–2). In the rest of that chapter, Paul shows the values that come when we align our lives with Christ.

You see, we don't have to guess, "What would Jesus do?" We can read God's Word and know for sure. When we find our center in the Bible, we learn what Jesus valued and the lifestyle that pleases God the most. Of course, many biblical values are countercultural. So be it. Christ was countercultural. In the face of obscenity He manifested purity. In the midst of evil He exemplified good.

Find your center in the Bible and you will find values that reflect heaven's values and will endure for eternity.

THE BIBLE IS YOUR CENTER
FOR BUILDING POSITIVE
FAMILY RELATIONSHIPS

Paul advised the Colossians about how to order their family relationships according to God's Word (Colossians 3:18–4:1). Here's what Paul wrote:

Wives

"Submit to your husbands, as is fitting in the Lord" (v. 18). The value of submission is also emphasized in Ephesians 5:22, Titus 2:4–5, and 1 Peter 3:1. In each case the word for *submit* is the same in the original language, meaning "to arrange under."[10] In each case, wives are to be submissive only to their own husbands, not to husbands in general. And in each case, there is an ethical reason for this submission—"as is fitting in the Lord"; "as to the Lord"; "so that no one will malign the word of God"; and that the husbands "may be won over without words by the behavior of their wives."

But biblical submission never implies inferiority. Paul said, "Now I want you to realize that the head of every man is Christ, and the head of the woman is man, and the head of Christ is God" (1 Corinthians 11:3). The wife is no more inferior to the husband than is Christ to the Father, but when Jesus came to earth, He voluntarily submitted His will to the Father's for the sake of accomplishing our redemption (Matthew 26:39; John 5:30; 6:38). The wife is asked to do the same to her husband for the sake of accomplishing God's will in the family.

Husbands

"Love your wives and do not be harsh with them" (v. 19). If a wife is to submit to her husband, he had better have her best interests at heart. The role of the husband, therefore, is to display the loving attitudes and actions toward his wife that make submission a redemptive act for everyone.

First Peter 3:7 changes the words but not the tone:

> Husbands, in the same way be considerate as you live with your wives, and treat them with respect as the weaker partner and as heirs with you of the gracious gift of life, so that nothing will hinder your prayers.

A husband should never underestimate the value of his wife, for "he who finds a wife finds what is good and receives favor from the LORD" (Proverbs 18:22).

Children

"Obey your parents in everything, for this pleases the Lord" (v. 20). Other adults can have a positive influence on our kids, but God assigns one set of parents to raise a child. It doesn't take a village; it takes a family.

While children are to obey their parents in everything, they are under no obligation to obey parents who ask them to steal, lie, prostitute their bodies, or behave in other morally reprehensible ways. Why would it please the Lord for children to obey parents who require things that He detests and are contrary to His will?

Jesus set the example for children by obeying Joseph and His mother, Mary. Luke 2:51 says, "Then he went down to Nazareth with them and was obedient to them." By the way, the word *obedient* is the same as *submit* in the case of the wife. Children are to arrange their agendas under the will of their parents. Many families today are held captive by the agenda of the children. One result is that personal relationships suffer. But when you place the Bible at the center of your family, you get it right.

8

THROUGH THE BIBLE, YOU FIND HOPE

*There is not enough darkness in all the world
to put out the light of one small candle.*

—ANONYMOUS

Missy was only fifteen and attractive, but she could never live up to the standards she set for herself. She thought she wasn't popular enough. She wasn't tall enough. And she definitely wasn't thin enough. The teen magazines she read created an unattainable image of the perfect body and the perfect life. And Missy became convinced that she would never look like those models on the covers. It was hopeless. Life was hopeless.

Missy knew her parents loved her, but she also believed they couldn't possibly understand. There was no way out. Missy simply ran out of hope.

Her suicide note was brief. It ended with the words "no hope."

When life turns out all wrong, where do you turn? When your marriage is on the rocks, can there be any hope? When your oncologist calls and wants to meet with you, what is the source of your strength? For too many people, there is no place to turn, no source of strength, *no hope.*

And no human can survive long without hope.

But what if you consistently connected with God through His Word? Would you find hope then? I'm talking about hope as a powerful conviction and life force, not just a passing feeling.

Yes, you would.

If you are having trouble finding God so that you can put your hope in Him, look for Him where He said He could be found—in the Bible. The Bible is God's repository of hope.

In the Bible, You Find "the God of Hope"

Hope is not an emotion that springs to life when things are going our way and strangely disappears the rest of the time. Hope is the cornerstone of life for those who have connected with God's heart.

"Why are you downcast, O my soul? Why so disturbed within me?" asked the psalmist. He then replied, "Put your hope in God" (Psalm 42:5; 43:5). "Blessed is he…whose hope is in the LORD his God, the Maker of heaven and earth" (Psalm 146:5–6).

God doesn't buy the idea of hopelessness because "with God all things are possible" (Matthew 19:26).

Paul prayed that the "God of hope" would fill his Christian friends at Rome "with all joy and peace." In fact, the apostle believed that by the power of the Holy Spirit these friends could "overflow with hope" (Romans 15:13).[1] He wanted them to experience a river of hope, and that's what God wants for you too.

The most important hope God brings to a hopeless world is His Son, your Savior. One of my favorite Christmas carols is *O Little Town of Bethlehem*. If you are battling a sense of hopelessness, think carefully about the first stanza. You've probably sung it hundreds of times, but have you noticed what it says?

> O little town of Bethlehem,
>   how still we see thee lie!
> Above thy deep and dreamless sleep
>   the silent stars go by;
> Yet in thy dark streets shineth the everlasting Light—
>   the hopes and fears of all the years
>   are met in thee tonight.

That night in Bethlehem, God met your fears with His hope—in the person of a baby born in a stable and laid in a manger. "For there is born to you this day in the city of David a Savior, who is Christ the Lord" (Luke 2:11, NKJV).

What kinds of hope will you find in God's Word? God provides hope for every kind of concern, every situation in life and death.

IN THE BIBLE, YOU FIND
A "LIVING HOPE"

Life is filled with challenges nasty and nice. Even when you choose to follow the Lord, those challenges continue—maybe even get nastier. So what kind of hope can you expect God to give you for life's challenges?

King David wrote, "LORD, you have assigned me my portion and my cup; you have made my lot secure. The boundary lines have fallen for me in pleasant places" (Psalm 16:5–6). The word *portion* means a share of something. When Joshua divided the Promised Land among the tribes of Israel, each tribe, each family, each person got a portion.

Imagine engaging in a hard-fought spiritual battle during your life. You withstand serious temptation, and you wonder if it has been worth it. Then you stand on the dais to receive your prize, and you discover, much to your eternal satisfaction, that your "portion" is the Lord Himself. He is the big prize and you've won Him.

That's what King David discovered. And it matters most when dark circumstances close in on us. David laments, "You are my refuge, my portion in the land of the living. Set me free from my prison, that I may praise your name…because of your goodness to me" (Psalm 142:5, 7).

John and Bobbi Bare went through dark times. John was a good man. He worked hard to provide for his family. But years ago, John's first wife suddenly left him, not for another man but for a woman. Bobbi hadn't fared much better. After years of marriage, her husband also walked out on her. Ironically, Bobbi's husband left her for another man.

Emotionally broken and spiritually bruised, John and Bobbi both lived lives of sorrow and self-imposed shame for years.

Then one day God in His grace brought them together and gave each one hope. It's as if God said to them, "I love you both very much. I know how tough your dark times have been. I want to reward your faithfulness to me with hope." John and Bobbi were both victims of sinful spouses. Now they are "prisoners of hope" (Zechariah 9:12). You should see them. The joy of the Lord is written all over their faces.[2]

For the Christian, Jesus Christ is our great prize. He gives us a "living hope," a hope that is now and forever alive (1 Peter 1:3–5).

IN THE BIBLE, YOU FIND A "DYING HOPE"

But God's Word reveals a hope that is strong enough for us to die by as well. And if there is any time when we need God's hope, it's when we're facing life's ultimate challenge.

The consistent teaching of God's Word is that the God who brings hope throughout our lives does so at the end of life as well: "The wicked is driven away in his wickedness: but the righteous hath hope in his death" (Proverbs 14:32, KJV).

Those in the Old Testament didn't fully understand what this hope entailed, but they had it nonetheless. In the New Testament, the writers filled in the blanks. Paul said, "If only for this life we have hope in Christ, we are to be pitied more than all men" (1 Corinthians 15:19). God's hope is like one of those bumper-to-bumper, seven-year/seventy-thousand-mile warranties on new cars—only better. The hope God gives begins at the crib side and carries on until the graveside.

With your hand in Jesus' hand, you don't have to face death alone. The Lord Jesus Christ is your hope and provides it when you need it most. Here's why that's true:

1. You can face death with One who has already experienced it.

Talk about an advantage. It's the difference between being a freshman football player in your first game and a senior who has played in two national championships. Experience— there's nothing like it.

If you want to face death without fear, place your hand in the hand of One who "suffered death, so that by the grace of God he might taste death for everyone" (Hebrews 2:9).

2. You can face death knowing that Jesus has taken away its sting.

Do you know what a scorpion without its stinger is? Supper for some elitist gourmets. What is a yellow jacket without its stinger? Just a brightly colored bug, not to be feared. That's the way death is without its sting.

Shortly before the fall of Israel in 722 B.C., God promised, "I will ransom them from the power of the grave; I will redeem them from death. Where, O death, are your plagues? Where, O grave, is your destruction?" (Hosea 13:14).

What God promised in the Old Testament, He performed in the New Testament. Paul triumphantly declares:

Then the saying that is written will come true: "Death has been swallowed up in victory." "Where, O death, is

your victory? Where, O death, is your sting?" The sting
of death is sin, and the power of sin is the law. But
thanks be to God! He gives us the victory through our
Lord Jesus Christ. (1 Corinthians 15:54–57)

The God of the Bible is the God of hope, and the God of
hope is the God of victory over death.

Does death cause pain? Sure it does. Does it hurt? You bet.
Just look at the red eyes at a funeral. So in what way has Jesus
taken away the sting of death? Simply this. Death is like a gun.
Guns don't kill people; bullets do. The gun is just the delivery
system. If you keep bullets from a gun, you take away the gun's
terror.

So it is with death. If it weren't for sin, death would have
no sting. People are afraid to die because they know they are
facing a day when God will square accounts. But for
Christians, our sin has already been paid for by the blood of
Jesus. We are confident that "there is now no condemnation
for those who are in Christ Jesus" (Romans 8:1). The gun is
still there, but the bullets are gone.

3. You can face death knowing it is not the end.

For most people death seems so final. After all, it's terminal,
isn't it?

Not in the least. We can face death with the confident
hope that there is more to come. Death is not the end....

It's just like Chicago.

Because I live in a smaller city, I have to fly through a
larger airport to catch a flight to the airport of my destination.

That usually means flying through Chicago's O'Hare International Airport. O'Hare is rarely my final destination. It's just a place where I change planes to go elsewhere. When I check my luggage in Lincoln, I check it to my final destination, not to Chicago. That's just a place I'm passing through.

Death will not be my end. It is not my final destination. I will only be changing bodies there (my next one will make this one seem pathetic). I will have already sent my luggage on ahead. Because I'm going on to heaven.

God's Word is the only document in the world that gives us a peek back into eternity past and forward into eternity future. It shows us that we can face death with hope, knowing it isn't the end. Our destination is a much better place. And Jesus is our Pilot.

IN THE BIBLE, YOU FIND A "RESURRECTION HOPE"

The idea of resurrection, coming alive again after we have died, has been around for a long time. It's not a uniquely Christian doctrine. The Old Testament is filled with verses that allude to the resurrection of the body. For example:

- Daniel 12:2: "Multitudes who sleep in the dust of the earth will awake: some to everlasting life, others to shame and everlasting contempt."
- Isaiah 26:19: "But your dead will live; their bodies will rise. You who dwell in the dust, wake up and shout for joy. Your dew is like the dew of the morning; the earth will give birth to her dead."

- Isaiah 25:8: "He will swallow up death forever. The Sovereign LORD will wipe away the tears from all faces." (This verse is the basis for both 1 Corinthians 15:54 and Revelation 21:4.)

But God gives us hope on the other side of death as well. What does "resurrection hope" mean? You could have dying hope and use it as a crutch, only to discover that death really was the end. But God rewards dying hope with the hope of resurrection. That's the reality of Job's words: "I know that my Redeemer lives, and that in the end he will stand upon the earth. And after my skin has been destroyed, yet in my flesh I will see God" (19:25–26).

You can face death with hope because Jesus already faced it—and beat it. The same is true with resurrection. Jesus has already blazed a trail ahead of you.

Have you ever stopped at a gas station to ask for directions? You know how frustrating it can be if you are not familiar with the area and a local gives you directions. "Go down the road to Culpepper's barn, and take a right after you pass where the grain silo used to be. After you go through the dip that flooded in '92, you'll see a road on the left. Take it."

It's almost impossible to follow directions like that. But what if the guy at the station said, "Hey, I've been over that road. Follow me. I'll take you there."

Jesus has already traveled the road ahead of us, and it makes all the difference. Jesus said, "Because I live, you also will live" (John 14:19). And Paul wrote, "But Christ has indeed been raised from the dead, the firstfruits of those who have fallen asleep [died]" (1 Corinthians 15:20). *Firstfruits* means there are more fruits of the resurrection to follow.

In the Bible, You Learn About "the Blessed Hope"

In Titus, Paul reveals yet another dimension to hope, where he writes about "the blessed hope—the glorious appearing of our great God and Savior, Jesus Christ" (2:13).

The promise of the blessed hope is that Christ will one day return to set up His kingdom. Time will end. Death will be no more. And those living at that time—like Elijah—will be snatched away to be with Christ. Paul described this in even more detail in 1 Corinthians 15:

> Listen, I tell you a mystery: We will not all sleep, but
> we will all be changed—in a flash, in the twinkling of
> an eye, at the last trumpet. For the trumpet will sound,
> the dead will be raised imperishable, and we will be
> changed. (vv. 51–52)

So how can the fact of our "blessed hope" change our lives today? Paul pointed to this hope as a compelling reason for every Christian to make the most of each day, denying wrong priorities and worldly lusts, all the while watching for Jesus to return. Why?

Jesus Christ could return at any time!

The Spring of Unfailing Hope

Are you feeling more hopeful about your future? According to a national poll taken by the University of Michigan Institute for Social Research, only one in five people report that they often feel hopeful about the future.[3] But the truth of the Bible can give us real, lasting hope.

I have a friend in Jamaica who owns an orchid farm. He listens to me on the radio, so every time I visit Jamaica I try to stop by and enjoy the beauty of his farm. As you might imagine, his orchids and other flowers are absolutely gorgeous! Everywhere you look you see displays of extravagant tropical beauty.

The secret of his lush harvest is an underground stream that rises out of the rocky ground and flows through his property, eventually to the ocean. The one-mile walk to the headwaters of that stream is well worth the time. There at the source, pure, cool spring water gushes furiously out of the ground—night and day, year in and year out, hundreds of gallons a minute of hope and promise for the waiting orchids downstream.

When I walk to those headwaters, I am reminded of the overflowing quality of God's hope. It is real and unfailing and abundant. Because of His hope, we can flourish today and walk into tomorrow without despair or fear.

The Bible tells us so.

9

THROUGH THE BIBLE, YOU LEARN DISTINCTIVE LIVING

A holy man is a mighty weapon in the hands of God.

—ROBERT MURRAY MCCHEYNE

IN THIS CHAPTER...

...enter the world of the culture wars.

...learn that character counts, but not enough.

...discover why purity is so important to God.

America is in a culture war, and things are not going well for our side.

Take one example—the so-called reality TV programs that have dominated American television for the past several years. They are nothing less than an invitation to voyeurism, concocting lifestyle situations that are foreign to biblical values (and probably to most Americans), while millions mindlessly watch.

Is some media elite in America bent on destroying all that most of us would deem good and holy? Many experts think so.[1] Those who seem to despise Judeo-Christian ethics are often in the positions of greatest influence in America—educators, intellectuals, Hollywood movie producers, TV personalities, and liberal politicians.

In his book *Culture Wars: The Struggle to Define America*,[2] James D. Hunter describes two sides of the conflict of ideologies:

- On the one side, he identifies the "orthodox" group—those who have a commitment to some definable, external, objective authority. From the perspective of the evangelical, this authority is God and His Holy Word.
- On the other side, Hunter finds the "progressives"—those who are more frequently given to rationalism and subjectivism. For them, truth is not an absolute but rather an unfolding reality of the way things are.

And caught in the middle more and more is the Bible.

USING (AND MISUSING) THE BIBLE AS A GUIDE FOR LIFE

Of course, whenever people appeal to the Bible for support in the cultural war, their arguments are meaningless to those who oppose God's standards. But recently we've seen the confusion that comes when people who hold positions foreign to God's Word *also* appeal to the Bible for support.

Nowhere was this more clearly illustrated than in the summer of 2003, when Rev. Gene Robinson was installed as the Bishop of the Episcopal diocese of New Hampshire.[3] This appointment would have drawn little attention outside New Hampshire's Episcopal church had Rev. Robinson not been openly gay for seventeen years. The fifty-four-year-old priest married in 1973 and fathered two daughters before divorcing his wife in 1986 and moving in with his gay lover.

When Matt Lauer of NBC's *Today* show (June 10, 2003) asked Rev. Robinson how he would respond to those in the Episcopal church who planned to leave the denomination as a result of his confirmation, Robinson responded, "I would say to them, you know what? This breaks God's heart that you would let something like this stand in the way of our commonness in the body of Christ."

How can those opposing Bishop Robinson and those supporting him *both* appeal to the Bible for support? I believe it's because people have chosen to use the Bible to support their point of view instead of trusting the Bible enough to let it change their point of view—and their way of life.

In this chapter, I want to explore what the Bible says about the distinctive lifestyle that is actually meant to be the norm for all those who follow Christ.

A DISTINCTIVELY BIBLICAL LIFE WILL AFFECT YOUR CHARACTER

Many educational institutions today are seeing the need to develop character in students. As a result, character education courses are springing up everywhere. Character education is an effort to develop virtues that are good for the individual and society. While most would agree that character education should be infused into the environment of education, not all agree on what character traits should be taught.

For example, the Character Education Network has identified the most common and broad-based group of character traits that it feels should be instilled in young people:[4]

THE CHARACTER EDUCATION NETWORK

RESPONSIBILITY—being accountable in word and deed. Having a sense of duty to fulfill tasks with reliability, dependability, and commitment.

PERSEVERANCE—pursuing worthy objectives with determination and patience while exhibiting fortitude when confronted with failure.

CARING—showing understanding of others by treating them with kindness, compassion, generosity, and a forgiving spirit.

SELF-DISCIPLINE—demonstrating hard work, controlling your emotions, words, actions, impulses, and desires. Giving your best in all situations.

CITIZENSHIP—being law abiding and involved in service to school, community, and country.

HONESTY—telling the truth, admitting wrongdoing. Being trustworthy and acting with integrity.

COURAGE—doing the right thing in the face of difficulty and following your conscience instead of the crowd.

FAIRNESS—practicing justice, equity, and equality; cooperating with one another. Recognizing the uniqueness and value of each individual within our diverse society.

RESPECT—showing high regard for an authority, other people, self, and country. Treating others as you would want to be treated. Understanding that all people have value as human beings.

Each of these character traits has roots in the Bible. But if you lived only by these character traits, would you be living distinctively according to God's Word?

Probably not. These traits are all people-centered, not God-centered. While they are commendable, they are not life-transforming and Holy Spirit–empowered, nor are they distinctively Christian. So while biblical character counts, it's just a beginning.

A Distinctively Biblical Life Will Affect Your Morals

Character needs a moral underpinning. Otherwise when the winds change, so will what we perceive as character. With the decline of the Bible's influence on popular culture has come a commensurate decline in morality. This trend has thrown fuel on the fires of our culture wars.

For example, George Barna noted:

> Americans unanimously denounced the September 11 terrorist attacks as a textbook example of evil, suggesting that there is a foundational belief in an absolute standard of right and wrong. Subsequent research, however, has shown that in the aftermath of the attacks, a minority of Americans believes in the existence of absolute moral truth.[5]

What's even more surprising is that less than one out of three born-again Christians believes in absolute moral truth.

Today, morality isn't based on the standard of God's Word but on the criterion of personal benefit. In a Barna poll conducted the day before the 9/11 attacks, when asked the basis on which they formed their moral choices, nearly half of all adults said they made their moral choices based on what would bring to them the most pleasing or satisfying results.[6]

Even so, Americans worry about declining morals. Three out of every four people say they are concerned about the moral condition of the United States. The stronger the respondents' personal faith, the stronger their concern. People who read the Bible were 32 percent more likely to be concerned than others.[7] Clearly, reading your Bible helps define what distinctive living is.

The Bible presents a comprehensive plan of morality—most notably, the Ten Commandments, the Levitical laws, and the teachings of Jesus. Still, in the current cultural wars, the Ten Commandments are often dismissed as a religious code unsuitable as an influence on contemporary moral choices.[8] The Levitical laws are scorned (for example, "Do not lie with a man as one lies with a woman; that is detestable," Leviticus 18:22) or are mangled by improper interpretation.[9] And the teachings of Jesus are selectively applied (for example, "I say to you that whoever looks at a woman to lust for her has already committed adultery with her in his heart," Matthew 5:28, NKJV).[10]

So while living a life of morality is a cut above living a life of character, something more than even morality is necessary if we are to live distinctive lives.

A DISTINCTIVELY BIBLICAL LIFE WILL AFFECT YOUR PURITY

The Bible indicates that if you want to connect with God, purity is a prerequisite. David asked, "Who may ascend the hill of the LORD? Who may stand in his holy place?" Who is prepared to enter the intimate presence of a Holy God? Who has the only chance of connecting with God? The king answered, "He who has clean hands and a pure heart" (Psalm 24:3–4).

But purity as a personal value is even rarer than morality these days.

Mr. Holland's Opus, which came out a few years ago, is a movie about a young, frustrated composer in Portland, Oregon, who takes a job as a high school band teacher in the 1960s. Although this diverts him from his lifelong goal of becoming a classical musician, Glenn Holland (played by Richard Dreyfuss) believes his school job will be temporary and will provide for his family.

At first he maintains his determination to write an opus, composing at his piano after putting in a full day teaching. But as life's demands increase, Mr. Holland knows that his dream of leaving a lasting musical legacy is dissipating.

Throughout the movie, Holland's relationship with his wife is strained, due in part to raising a deaf son. While directing the school musical, the middle-aged teacher becomes intrigued by the musical skill and physical beauty of a senior named Rowena. When he affirms her abilities, Rowena becomes attracted to him, telling him that she has decided to move to New York City to pursue her own dreams and that she wants him to go with her. It would be Holland's chance to feel young again and his ticket out of the humdrum life of a high school music teacher. Maybe he would even write his magnum opus.

After the final performance of the school musical, Mr. Holland rendezvous with Rowena at the local drug store, where the bus picks up passengers. Her eyes light up as she sees him approach, but she quickly notices that he has no luggage.

"You pack light," she jests.

Mr. Holland hands Rowena a piece of paper with the names of some people he knows in New York where she could stay.

"This isn't the way I imagined it," Rowena sighs.

"But it's the best way," Holland says, as he finds the inner strength to resist temptation and remain pure.

That evening, Glenn Holland enters his bedroom, where his wife appears to be sleeping. He looks at her tenderly and says, "I love you." To his surprise, his wife looks up at him and responds, "I know." Mr. Holland takes his wife in his arms and holds her tightly. This scene lasts approximately four and a half minutes (which in Hollywood time is an eternity).[11]

Do you know what caught everyone by surprise about this movie? It was Mr. Holland's choice for purity, for loyalty to his marriage vows—and that this choice was presented as a worthy life "opus." That choice was quite a shock in a world where purity is all but passé.

What can you do to ensure that you have clean hands and a pure heart? Three things come to mind immediately.

1. Be disgusted with sin.

Already I fear I've lost some of you. In our postmodern era, tolerance is chief among virtues. We make room for almost every lifestyle or perversion as an acceptable part of life. But the Bible reveals that sin sickens God, and if you want to live in harmony with Him, it must sicken you as well.

While the Bible teaches us to love our enemies, it also says that God hates evil.[12] David wrote: "You are not a God who takes pleasure in evil; with you the wicked cannot dwell. The arrogant cannot stand in your presence; you hate all who do wrong" (Psalm 5:4–5).

Purity is one of the marks of a distinctive life. As the psalmist wrote, "Because I consider all your precepts right, I hate every wrong path" (Psalm 119:128). Tolerance in the twenty-first century is not distinctive; purity is.

2. Keep short accounts with God.

Keeping short accounts with God means you don't let your sin pile up, day after day, planning to deal with it at some time in the future. Each day you take your sin to God in broken-ness and confession. It becomes a daily habit of life for those who would live distinctively.

What happens if you don't deal with personal sin consis-tently, daily, almost hourly?

For one thing, you forget about it. It passes from your mind—but not from God's. For another, unconfessed sin has a numbing effect on your mind and spirit. You become less dis-gusted by it. You begin to say, "Oh, it's not so bad." But that's rationalization, not confession.

Fortunately, we can always come to the altar of confession because God's Word promises, "If we confess our sins, he is faithful and just and will forgive us our sins and purify us from all unrighteousness" (1 John 1:9). That's good news for all of us.

3. Ask the Holy Spirit to fill the void.

When you are broken by your sin and confess it to God, He "hits the delete key," and that sin is expunged from your record. But then you have a blank screen, an empty file. Nature hates a vacuum; if you leave your file empty, other sins will rush in to fill it. So ask the Holy Spirit to fill the void instead (Ephesians 5:18).

That brings me to my final point about distinctive living.

A DISTINCTIVELY BIBLICAL LIFE IS MADE POSSIBLE BY THE HOLY SPIRIT

The Bible reveals an important paradox about the Christian life: *Even though we must choose to follow God with all our heart, soul, mind, and body, it's not really us who does the living—it's the Holy Spirit of God who lives through us!*

Paul put his finger on it when he said, "I have been crucified with Christ and I no longer live, but Christ lives in me. The life I live in the body, I live by faith in the Son of God, who loved me and gave himself for me" (Galatians 2:20). It is the power of the living Christ that enables us to live distinctively.

Distinctive living, then, is living in the power of God's

Spirit and exhibiting the fruit of His presence in our lives. Some of that fruit is mentioned in Galatians 5:22–23: love, joy, peace, patience, kindness, goodness, faithfulness, gentleness, and self-control. Anything less isn't complete Christian living at all. So those who claim to have faith in Christ but whose lives reflect no change are only fooling themselves. A new creation in Christ abandons old heroes, old habits, and old hangouts because all things have become new (2 Corinthians 5:17).

But the Holy Spirit gives us guidance and comfort as well as power. When Jesus was nearing the end of His ministry on earth, He made a pledge to His disciples: "And I will ask the Father, and he will give you another Counselor to be with you forever—the Spirit of truth" (John 14:16–17).

Jesus' promise to us is the same. He has not left us orphans. The Holy Spirit has taken His place in our midst to do Christ's work through us. "But the Counselor, the Holy Spirit, whom the Father will send in my name, will teach you all things and will remind you of everything I have said to you" (John 14:26).

Distinctive living is "Spirit living." Without divine help, holy living is just a dream. Evangelist D. L. Moody said, "You might as well try to hear without ears, or breathe without lungs, as try to live a Christian life without the Spirit of God in your heart."

LET GOD REMAKE YOU

Two verses that most encourage me on this subject are Romans 12:1–2. J. B. Phillips's compelling translation reads:

With eyes wide open to the mercies of God, I beg
you, my brothers, as an act of intelligent worship, to
give him your bodies, as a living sacrifice, consecrated
to him and acceptable by him. Don't let the world
around you squeeze you into its own mould, but let
God re-make you so that your whole attitude of mind
is changed. Thus you will prove in practice that the
will of God's good, acceptable to him and perfect.

The culture wars will continue and deepen. But there is
hope. We *can* live distinctively as individuals and as communities, believing in—and working toward—the victory of right
over wrong.

Where do we start? By looking to the pages of the Bible
as the measure of the truly good life, and by reaching for the
power of God as our only means to attain it.

Four Amazing Bible Discoveries

Part Three of this book outlines four amazing discoveries that will revolutionize your understanding of God's Word. These are not secrets but simply overlooked truths that will enhance your ability to connect with God.

Are you ready for some surprises? Here's one: Half the books of the Bible can be read in less time than it takes to watch the evening news.

It's true. Read on, and I'll show you what I mean.

10

THE BIBLE IS LIVING HISTORY

*The hinge of history is found on
the door of a Bethlehem stable.*
—ANONYMOUS

IN THIS CHAPTER...

...view an amazing
time line of
history.

...uncover how
Bible history is
woven into world
history.

...find out how to
connect with the
God of history.

When I was a high school student, Mrs. Aiken was what I thought of when I thought of "old." How old she really was I never knew, but to this sixteen-year-old, Mrs. Aiken looked positively ancient. She taught ancient history and Latin—probably because she lived through the one and grew up speaking the other.

Actually I'm not sure Mrs. Aiken liked either history or Latin. For her, history class consisted of passing along endless lists of emperors' names, important dates, the who went to war against whom (most we dubbed the "Who Cares Wars"). I can still hear her droning through a history reading as if she were going down a list of plague victims.

Maybe I was from a different planet than Mrs. Aiken, but history always fascinated me. Sure, the details could be boring, but I loved hearing about people living millennia ago who weren't so different from us. I also enjoyed discovering how important cultures developed independently from each other around the world, yet showed such amazing parallels.

PARALLEL HISTORY

Let me show you what I mean. Following are four short historical sketches. Give them a quick read. Then I have a surprise for you.

A Mayan story

"My name is Pok. I live in Mesoamerica, in the highlands of the Yucatan Peninsula. My people are the Maya. We have been dominated by the Olmec for more than a thousand years, but one day my people will be a great people.

"The Maya are very religious. We have small temple-pyramids, but one day we hope to build the greatest pyramids in the world. I can't imagine pyramids anywhere that could equal what the men of my village are planning.

"My friends and I spend most of our free time watching the men play pok-a-tok. It's a Mayan ball game, played on a huge court with stone rings high on the wall on either side of the court. The object is to get the ball through the stone ring, without getting yourself killed.

"The weather is warm here, but sometimes I wrap myself in my huipel, our traditional Mayan cotton dress, go to the cenote to draw water, and wonder. I wonder if there are still people living back where my ancestors came from before they crossed the great and terrible cold to find these lush jungles. I wonder if they play pok-a-tok. I could ask the Ah Kin, our high priest, but his answers never satisfy me. Still, I wonder."

A Chinese story

"My name is Yang-tzu, and in my seventy-eight years I have seen much change in my China. We are a proud people, inventors of more things than you can shake a chopstick at. But things are changing.

"Hundreds of years ago the Xia ruled our land, but then the Shang came. They were mighty warriors but became morally corrupt. My people, the Chou, are virtuous, especially our national hero, King Wen, and his son, King Wu. Because we follow the moral ways of heaven, we were successful in overthrowing the Shang. Now the Chou rule by t'ien ming, the 'Mandate of Heaven.'

"But as I said, things are changing in my country. About fifty years ago, just as Ling and I were about to be married, northern barbarians overran our western cities and captured our capital, Hao, near Xi'an. Chinese philosophy and culture are flowering, but morally we are becoming like the Shang.

"I constantly cry out to T'ien, the sky god, the king of gods, to bring justice to our land, but he is silent. Why doesn't he remove t'ien ming and restore our land? Is he not a god as I have believed?"

An Egyptian story

"I am Tefnakht, great chief of the Meshwesh, Pharaoh of all Egypt. Well, that may be a bit of a stretch. In my day, there is not one pharaoh over all Egypt.

"My Egypt is divided into three parts: the Delta, ruled by the pharaohs of Bubastis; Middle Egypt, stretching from south of the Delta to Asyut and governed by the princes of Herakleopolis; and Upper Egypt, administered by the priests of Amen and the Wife of God. I rule in the Delta, at Sais, about as close to the Great Sea as you can get.

"I suppose you should know that I'm not really Egyptian. I am Libyan. The Meshwesh are a warring people. Mercenaries we are and proud of it. We practice no trade but war. Sheshonq I, king of the twenty-second Dynasty, supported Israel's king Jeroboam against King Solomon's son, Rehoboam. We don't care who we fight for or against, as long as the money is right.

"You're welcome to come to my house anytime. I'll hold an extravagant party in your honor. We'll have singers, dancers, and acrobats. Or if you like, we'll just play a quiet board game like Hounds and Jackals, or Senet. But be advised. I am first and foremost a soldier, a mercenary. I hear now that the king of Israel may need some military muscle against Assyria. If he asks and can pay, I'm there."

An Indian story

"I live with my family on the rich farmland along the Ganges River. My name is Chupta Vaisha, and my people are Aryan. Aryans came from Central Asia and swept into the Indus Valley through the fabled Khyber Pass almost a thousand years ago, driving out the Harappan.

"Since my people were originally nomads and warlords, making the switch to agriculture was not easy. But the land is good and water is plentiful. Our houses are made of straw and wood, but we have proven ourselves to be quite ingenious plumbers. We have giant reservoirs for fresh water and drainage systems that feed running water directly into our houses.

"I'm sorry to say that dark clouds are on the horizon for my land. When my father was a boy, our people began to develop a caste system, which grows in strength every year. I am a farmer so I belong to the Vaishya, the caste of traders and farmers. Beneath us are the Shudra, the workers. But immediately above us are the Kshatriya, the warriors, and the highest caste are the Brahmana, the priests.

"But if you come to my house, I will treat you well. In the evening I can read the Vedas, our sacred poems and hymns. You can meet my friends around the Yagna, our central village fireplace, where we share news of the day. I think you'd like my village."

Bridging the time line of history

Why did I tell you these stories? While the stories you just read are not historical, they do fall into the realm of historical plausibility. If they were true, they would accurately reflect life in each of these distant societies.

Now for the surprise I promised you: *Each story reflects what was happening in different parts of the world at the same time. If they had taken place, they would have taken place simultaneously.*

What's more, we could even peg them to a Bible event: *Had these stories been historical, each of them would have taken place while the ten northern tribes of Israel were falling into the hands of the Assyrians in the year 722 B.C.*

The Bible says, "The king of Assyria invaded the entire land, marched against Samaria and laid siege to it for three years. In the ninth year of Hoshea, the king of Assyria captured Samaria and deported the Israelites to Assyria" (2 Kings 17:5–6).

That's what we know from the Bible. But the four sketches show what could have been happening in other places in the world in the same year.

Too many people today assume that all or most of what they read in the Bible occurred in some make-believe biblical story land (while assuming that everything they read in a history book happened in the "real world"). But the Bible is a factual book. Bible events really happened, and they happened while other things were occuring in different places in the world.

Now here's how this perspective can help you: One of the best ways to discover God in His Word is to discover Him as the God of history. If we fail to bridge the time line of history with the time line of the Bible, we'll fail to connect the God of the Bible with the God of history.

By laying the time line of the Bible over the time line of history, we come to understand the Bible much better and respond to the God of the Bible with a much more vigorous faith.

But before we do that, let's find out how much you know of history.

Take the Time Line Quiz

Every good detective story or TV drama features the methodical piecing together of bits of evidence. That's one of the secrets behind the phenomenal success of the TV series *CSI: Crime Scene Investigation*. The whole program is about gathering and interpreting forensic evidence at crime scenes.

How are you at piecing together historical evidence? Answer each question in this fun Time Line Quiz as true or false.

Time Line Quiz—True or False

___ The Sumerian civilization in Mesopotamia, the Egyptian civilization in North Africa, and the Mayan civilization in Central America all developed at approximately the same time.

___ Civilizations were already flourishing in Mexico and China when Moses was born in Egypt.

___ Although many think the Trojan War was waged during classical Greek times, it was actually fought nearly two centuries before David fought Goliath.

___ The first Olympic Games were held more than fifty years before the Northern Kingdom was carried into Assyrian captivity.

___ Homer wrote *The Iliad* and *The Odyssey* before many of the books of the Old Testament were written.

___ When Moses was born in Egypt, the great pyramids had already cast their shadow over the plains of Giza for more than one thousand years.

___ The Romans built the Appian Way more than one hundred years before the Chinese built their Great Wall.

___ Jerusalem and Beijing were founded about the same time.

___ Native Americans migrated from northern Asia across the Bering Strait just after Abraham and his family migrated from Ur of the Chaldees to Canaan.

___ Lao-Tsu (founder of Taoism), Siddhartha Gautama (founder of Buddhism), and Confucius (founder of Confucianism) were born within about fifty years of each other, but more than a thousand years before Mohammed (founder of Islam).

Believe it or not, the answer to each question is "true." I hope that fitting these pieces together will help you appreciate the Bible even more.

Now use the following historical time line to help you see how the dates in Bible history coordinate with the rest of history. I've grouped dates to help you compare the sequence of biblical events with what was happening elsewhere in the world at approximately the same time.

TIME LINE OF BIBLICAL HISTORY

3100 B.C.	Menes unites Upper and Lower Egypt in one kingdom
2750 B.C.	Sumerian civilization begins at Ur; Phoenicians found Tyre
2600 B.C.	Pre-Mayan civilization begins in Mesoamerica
2540 B.C.	The Great Sphinx of Egypt is built
2091 B.C.	Abraham, Terah, and family leave Ur
2000 B.C.	Stonehenge is built in England
1950 B.C.	Native Americans migrate from Asia
1766 B.C.	Shang Dynasty in China begins
1526 B.C.	Moses born in Egypt
1500 B.C.	Mexican Sun Pyramid built; Aryans invade India
1446 B.C.	The Exodus from Egypt
1323 B.C.	King Tut dies in Egypt
1183 B.C.	Troy destroyed during the Trojan War
1051 B.C.	Saul crowned Israel's first king
1011 B.C.	David crowned king of Israel
1000 B.C.	Beijing built; California Indians construct wood-reed houses
930 B.C.	Hebrew Kingdom divided into Israel and Judah
900 B.C.	Celts invade Britain
869 B.C.	Elijah defeats the prophets of Baal on Mt. Carmel
850 B.C.	Homer writes *The Iliad* and *The Odyssey*
776 B.C.	First Olympic Games held in Greece
765 B.C.	Amos prophesies in Israel

753 B.C.	Hosea marries Gomer, prophesies in Israel
753 B.C.	Rome founded by Romulus and Remus
740 B.C.	Micah begins prophetic ministry in Israel
740 B.C.	The year King Uzziah died, Isaiah received vision from God
722 B.C.	Samaria falls; Israel captured by Assyrian King Sargon II
604 B.C.	Lao-tzu, founder of Taoism, is born
600 B.C.	Phoenicians make a three-year voyage around Africa
587 B.C.	Nebuchadnezzar sacks Jerusalem, destroys Solomon's temple
563 B.C.	Buddha (Siddhartha Gautama), founder of Buddhism, is born
560 B.C.	Aesop, Greek author, writes his famed fables
551 B.C.	Confucius, Chinese founder of Confucianism, is born
550 B.C.	Temple of Diana built, one of the Seven Wonders of the World
539 B.C.	Cyrus the Great captures Babylon, releases Jews
536 B.C.	Zerubbabel leads first return from Babylon to Jerusalem
478 B.C.	Esther (Hadassah) becomes Queen of Persia
469 B.C.	Socrates, premier philosopher of ancient Greece, is born
455 B.C.	Ezra leads second return from Babylon to Jerusalem
445 B.C.	Nehemiah leads third return from Babylon to Jerusalem
396 B.C.	Malachi completes his prophecy, Old Testament ends
331 B.C.	Alexander the Great conquers the Persian Empire
312 B.C.	Romans build the Appian Way from Rome to Capua
5 B.C.	Jesus Christ, founder of Christianity, Son of God, is born
4 B.C.	Herod the Great dies
A.D. 23	Pliny the Elder, who wrote *Natural History,* is born
A.D. 30	Jesus Christ crucified, buried, and raised from the dead
A.D. 35	Saul of Tarsus converted to Christ
A.D. 37	Flavius Josephus, Jewish historian for Roman Empire, is born
A.D. 43	London founded as a city
A.D. 55	Tacitus, Roman historian who wrote *Annals,* is born
A.D. 68	The apostle Paul beheaded by Emperor Nero near Rome
A.D. 70	Jerusalem sacked and burned by Emperor Titus
A.D. 95	The apostle John writes the book of Revelation

It's not hard to see how the events recorded in the Bible—and other dates important to Christians—run like a red thread of redemption through time. And you and I can be confident that, whatever might be in the day's headlines, God will continue to act in history until everything He has promised is fulfilled. King Nebuchadnezzar saw the truth of God's hand behind even his great empire when he learned that "the Most High rules in the kingdom of men, gives it to whomever He will, and sets over it the lowest of men" (Daniel 4:17, NKJV).

THE STORY BEHIND THE NUMBERS

Now think about the spread of years between these people and/or events:

- Had Abraham migrated from Ur of the Chaldees to England rather than to Canaan, he could have been a tourist at Stonehenge.
- Aesop wrote his famous fables before the Old Testament books of Ezra, Nehemiah, Esther, Daniel, Haggai, Zechariah, and Malachi were written.
- Almost twenty-one centuries before Columbus "sailed the ocean blue," Phoenicians undertook a three-year voyage around Africa.
- Abraham lived as many years on the other side of Jesus Christ as we live on this side of Him.
- The Greeks held their first Olympic Games before either the Northern Kingdom or Southern Kingdom disappeared.

Think about these contemporary people or events:

- The apostle Paul was a contemporary of three famous historians: Pliny the Elder, Flavius Josephus, and Tacitus.
- The Greek epic poet Homer and the Jewish epic prophet Elijah were contemporaries.
- Socrates and Queen Esther were contemporaries.
- While the Greeks were fighting the people of Troy in the Trojan War, the Israelites were fighting everyone around them in the period of the Judges.

Now think about these numbers:

- 40—the approximate number of years between Jesus' crucifixion and Paul's beheading.
- 657—the years between the destruction of Jerusalem by the Babylonians and the city's destruction by the Romans.
- 1100—the number of years after Saul of Israel became king that Saul of Tarsus became an apostle of Jesus Christ.
- 3932—the year on the Chinese calendar when Marco Polo returned from China in A.D. 1295 to tell his tales of the Far East.
- 4000—the approximate number of years between the building of palace ziggurats and the destruction of Saddam Hussein's palaces during the recent Iraq War at the same location.

Okay, so now you know some history trivia to e-mail to your friends. But that's not my reason for sharing these facts. I want you to see that God is at work in history and that the biblical record is a reliable part of a larger picture.[1]

CONNECTING WITH THE
GOD OF HISTORY

How does placing biblical history within the wider context of world history help you find God in the Bible? Let me suggest some ways:

God is God over all nations.

When you see how the Bible's time line parallels history, you will see a much bigger God than you may have imagined growing up.

The Bible presents Yahweh, the God of Israel, as the one true God, the God of heaven and earth. When Abraham was pleading with God for the souls of the sinful Sodomites, he asked rhetorically, "Will not the Judge of all the earth do right?" (Genesis 18:25).

When the priests carried the ark across the Jordan River, Joshua said that they were carrying the ark belonging to "the Lord of all the earth" (Joshua 3:13). You see, Joshua knew that He who was God on Israel's side of the river was also God on Jericho's side.

When you overlay biblical history on world history, you get a clearer picture that God is not a small-town God, or the God of a small Middle Eastern country.

He is a big God—the God of all the earth.

God is God over all time.

God is not an idle spectator to world politics. Hannah understood this: "The LORD sends poverty and wealth; he humbles and he exalts" (1 Samuel 2:7). Asaph understood it: "It is God who judges: He brings one down, he exalts another" (Psalm 75:7). So did Solomon: "The king's heart is in the hand of the LORD; he directs it like a watercourse wherever he pleases" (Proverbs 21:1).

When you read history through the eyes of the Bible, you see that God is in control of what's happening all over the world. God knows what He's doing, even when murderous dictators despoil their own people. God has a plan for the ages, and He works His plan according to His own timetable.

So if things aren't working out quite like you think the Bible predicts, don't abandon your faith in God. Just adjust your clock.

WATCH HOW GOD PREPARES THE WAY

One of the great benefits of reading history through the Bible is that you become aware that God prepares people, places, and events in advance to accomplish His will. Look at this divine-historical phenomenon at work in God's preparing the way for the Messiah to be born in Bethlehem (as prophesied in Micah 5:2).

With the tragic death of Julius Caesar in 27 B.C., Caesar's nephew Octavian became emperor and allowed himself to be called "the revered one," or *augustus* in Latin. Thus he became Caesar Augustus.

Soon he wanted to know how many subjects he had, and that required a census.

In those days Caesar Augustus issued a decree that a
census should be taken of the entire Roman world.
And everyone went to his own town to register. So
Joseph also went up from the town of Nazareth in
Galilee to Judea, to Bethlehem the town of David,
because he belonged to the house and line of David.
While they were there, the time came for the baby to
be born, and she gave birth to her firstborn, a son.
(Luke 2:1, 3–4, 6–7)

What would cause Joseph and Mary to make the arduous
journey to Bethlehem when she was so far along in her preg-
nancy? The decree of the emperor would! But God's timetable
determined man's history.

Yet no census would have even been taken had there been
no Roman Empire. While Micah was predicting that Messiah
would be born in Bethlehem (5:2) and Isaiah was predicting
that "the virgin will be with child and will give birth to a son,
and will call him Immanuel" (7:14), God was preparing the
somewhat unimpressive beginnings of an empire.

According to legend, only a dozen or so years before
Micah's and Isaiah's prophecies, twin brothers Romulus and
Remus founded the city of Rome (753 B.C.). Think of it—
Isaiah and Micah couldn't possibly have known that from
what was a tiny village in their day would come the empire
God would use to fulfill their prophecies!

So never again assume that the history of the Bible is some
separate, spiritual, supernatural history. It is simply the record
of God working in the lives of His people and in our world.
And when world history is overlaid on Bible history, they pro-
duce a synchronized whole.

CONNECTING WITH THE GOD OF TIME

The fact is, God has *never* been disconnected from this world. Or from you. He is just as involved in your world and your everyday affairs as He has been from the beginning of time.

And even more important, the God who was sovereignly at work in our past is the same God who will be Lord of our future. After all, prophecy is just history yet to happen. If you can trace God's movement in history past, you can trust His motivations for history future too.

11

THE BIBLE IS A LETTER TO YOU

Put it before them briefly so they will read it, clearly so they will appreciate it, picturesquely so they will remember it, and above all, accurately so they will be guided by its light.

—JOSEPH PULITZER

IN THIS CHAPTER...

...learn to take a different look at the Bible.

...see what a letter from the first century looked like.

...compare the Bible to other texts of its time.

You might as well be from Mars. That's how some people look at you when you tell them you believe the Bible. "How could a rational person believe all those myths and legends in the Bible?" they ask. "Does anything in the Bible have the ring of historical authenticity?"

Well, yes, it does, actually. And in this chapter I'll show you what I mean. Of course, with a little time and patience, you could approach the issue of authenticity from many other angles: archaeological data, documentary proofs, and internal evidences, for example. You could even make a strong case for the Bible by looking at how its impact on individual lives and our entire world is unparalleled and (apart from God) unexplainable.

But my purpose in this chapter is to look at one surprising body of evidence—the testimony of Bible letters.

Ultimately, the authenticity of the Bible is a matter of faith, as is the authenticity of anything else beyond the reach of personal confirmation. But faith in the Bible's authenticity is *not* irrational—like driving your car seventy-five miles per hour on a fog-enshrouded freeway. Faith in the Bible is a personal choice that rests on a substantial foundation.

HOW RELIABLE ARE BIBLE DOCUMENTS?

Scholars judge the authenticity of an ancient text by the number of copies available to scrutinize and by the age of the earliest copies. This is called the *manuscript evidence*:

- The greater the number of copies, the greater the likelihood of authenticity.
- The older the copies, the greater the likelihood of authenticity.
- And, the fewer years between the original writing and the earliest copy, the greater the likelihood of authenticity.

Look at the chart below, which compares available New Testament manuscripts with those of contemporary authors.[1]

Author	Date of Writing	Number of Copies	Date of Earliest Copy	Time Between Writing and Earliest Copy
Herodotus	480–425 B.C.	8	A.D. 900	1300 years
Thucydides	460–400 B.C.	8	A.D. 900	1300 years
Caesar	100–44 B.C.	10	A.D. 900	1000 years
New Testament	A.D. 40–100	24,000	A.D. 125	25 years
Suetonius	A.D. 75–160	8	A.D. 930	800 years
Tacitus	A.D. 100	10	A.D. 1100	1000 years

People don't routinely question the authenticity of Thucydides, the Greek historian, or Herodotus, the Persian historian. And yet the time of writing between each man and the earliest copy we have of their writings is about thirteen hundred years. But in the case of New Testament manuscripts, only about twenty-five years passed between their writing and the first copies scholars have to examine.[2]

Then there's the sheer volume of New Testament manuscript copies available—about twenty-four thousand—for scholars to scrutinize. Remember, the more copies, the greater the likelihood of authenticity. Now look at the number of copies of Thucydides and Herodotus. It's hard to miss the strength of the evidence in favor of the Bible's authenticity.

When you compare the Bible with other literary works of the same time period, then, the Bible's authenticity shines through. Therefore, we can approach God with confidence through the pages of His Word because we can trust that our manuscript sources are historically valid.

But what about the Bible's *internal, literary evidence*?

Some people think the Bible is written in a secret code that they can't understand. But the truth is, it is written in the accepted literary genres of its day, such as history, essay, and personal story. God took the normal forms of written communication and used them to convey what was on His mind. (And then He made certain it was the most published book in world history!)

Now let's examine more closely one type of literary genre in the Bible—the letter.

LETTERS FROM LONG AGO

Suppose you could climb into a time machine and transport yourself back to the time of David or Hezekiah or Nehemiah. You would expect to find ordinary letters passing between people in those days. But what would they look like? How would they read?

The following chart identifies where in the Old Testament a letter is mentioned, the person who sent it, the one who received it, and whether or not the full text of the letter is recorded in the pages of the Bible.

LETTERS OF THE OLD TESTAMENT

SCRIPTURE	SENDER	RECIPIENT	FULL TEXT
2 Samuel 11:14–15	David	Joab	No
1 Kings 5:3–6	Solomon	Hiram	Yes
1 Kings 5:8–9	Hiram	Solomon	Yes
2 Kings 5:6	King of Aram	King of Israel	Yes
2 Kings 10:2–3	Jehu	Ahab's officers	Yes
2 Kings 10:5	Ahab's officers	Jehu	Yes
2 Kings 10:6	Jehu	Ahab's officers	Yes

Scripture	Sender	Recipient	Full Text
2 Kings 18:19–25	the Rabshakeh	Hezekiah	Yes
2 Kings 19:10–13	Sennacherib	Hezekiah	Yes
2 Kings 20:12	Merodach-Baladan	Hezekiah	No
2 Chronicles 2:3–10	Solomon	Hiram	Yes
2 Chronicles 2:11–16	Hiram	Solomon	Yes
2 Chronicles 21:12–15	Elijah	Jehoram	Yes
2 Chronicles 30:6–9	Hezekiah	people of Judah	Yes
2 Chronicles 32:10–15	Sennacherib	people of Jerusalem	Yes
2 Chronicles 32:17	Sennacherib	people of Jerusalem	Yes
Ezra 4:8–16	Rehum and Shimshai	Artaxerxes	Yes
Ezra 4:17–23	Artaxerxes	Rehum and Shimshai	Yes
Ezra 5:6–17	Tattenai	Darius	Yes
Ezra 6:2–12	Cyrus	Ecbatana file	Yes
Ezra 7:12–26	Artaxerxes	Ezra	Yes
Nehemiah 2:7–9	Nehemiah	Artaxerxes	No
Nehemiah 6:2	Sanballat and Geshum	Nehemiah	Yes
Nehemiah 6:3	Nehemiah	Sanballat and Geshum	Yes
Nehemiah 6:6–7	Sanballat	Nehemiah	Yes
Nehemiah 6:8	Nehemiah	Sanballat	Yes
Nehemiah 6:17	Nobles of Judah	Tobiah	No
Nehemiah 6:17	Tobiah	Nobles of Judah	No
Nehemiah 6:19	Tobiah	Nehemiah	No
Esther 1:22	Xerxes	Persian kingdom	No
Esther 3:13–14	Xerxes	Persian kingdom	No
Esther 8:5–10	Mordecai	Satraps, governors	No
Esther 9:20	Mordecai	Persian Jews	No
Esther 9:25	Xerxes	Persian kingdom	No
Esther 9:29	Esther and Mordecai	Persian Jews	No
Isaiah 37:9–13	Sennacherib	Hezekiah	Yes
Isaiah 37:22–35	Isaiah	Hezekiah	Yes
Isaiah 38:9–20	Hezekiah	everyone	Yes
Jeremiah 29:4–23	Jeremiah	Exile survivors	Yes
Jeremiah 29:25–28	Jeremiah	Shemaiah	Yes
Jeremiah 29:31–32	Jeremiah	Exile survivors	Yes
Daniel 4:1–37	Nebuchadnezzar	to all people	Yes

That body of evidence is pretty impressive. Even most Bible students have no idea how many letters are found in the Old Testament. But I'm glad so many are included, because common letters give us insight into people's hearts, their interests and beliefs, and their lives.

PERSON-TO-PERSON IN THE ROMAN EMPIRE

It really wasn't until the rise of the Roman Empire that letter writing became common. People like Cicero, Seneca, and Pliny the Younger wrote a wide spectrum of letters, sometimes spontaneously composed and other times written for publication. Letters contained news from home, introductions of friends, and financial advice. Pliny even wrote with enthusiasm about his country house and property.[3]

The Roman postal system was called the *cursus publicus*. Riders on a relay carried a letter as far as 170 miles in twenty-four hours.[4] In less than a week, a letter could cross the Empire. The Roman government, however, provided postal service only for official documents.

Private letters were usually carried personally. Thus the apostles would seek out faithful and trustworthy Christian friends to carry their epistles to their destinations. Tychicus was such a person. He apparently carried Paul's letter to the Ephesians (Ephesians 6:21) and the one to the Colossians (Colossians 4:7). The epistle to Philemon was also sent at this time.

In the last chapter of Romans, Paul commends to the church at Rome a businesswoman by the name of Phoebe, with whom he sent his epistle to them. Apparently Phoebe had business in Rome, and Paul seized the opportunity to send his most important letter along with her.

Twenty-one of the twenty-seven books of the New Testament are letters. Check out some examples:

LETTERS OF THE NEW TESTAMENT

Scripture	Sender	Recipient	Full Text
Acts 9:2	High Priest	Saul of Tarsus	No
Acts 15:23–30	Jerusalem council	Antioch church	Yes
Acts 22:5	High Priest	Saul of Tarsus	No
Acts 23:25–30	Commander	Claudius Lysias	Yes
Acts 28:21	Judean Jews	Roman Jews	No
Romans 1:1, 7	Paul	Roman church	Yes
1 Corinthians 1:1–2	Paul	Corinthian church	Yes
1 Corinthians 5:9	Paul	Corinthian church	No
1 Corinthians 16:3	Paul	Corinthian men	No
2 Corinthians 1:1–2	Paul	Corinthian church	Yes
2 Corinthians 2:4	Paul	Corinthian church	No
2 Corinthians 3:1	Corinthian church	Paul	No
2 Corinthians 7:8	Paul	Corinthian church	No
2 Corinthians 10:9	Paul	Corinthian church	No
2 Corinthians 10:10	Paul	Corinthian church	No
2 Corinthians 10:11	Paul	Corinthian church	No
Galatians 1:1–2	Paul	Galatian churches	Yes
Galatians 6:11	Paul	Galatian churches	No
Ephesians 1:1–2	Paul	Ephesian church	Yes
Philippians 1:1–2	Paul	Philippian church	Yes
Colossians 1:1–2	Paul	Colossian church	Yes
1 Thessalonians 1:1	Paul	Thessalonians	Yes
2 Thessalonians 1:1	Paul	Thessalonians	Yes
2 Thessalonians 2:2	Paul	Thessalonians	No
1 Timothy 1:1–2	Paul	Timothy	Yes
2 Timothy 1:1–2	Paul	Timothy	Yes

SCRIPTURE	SENDER	RECIPIENT	FULL TEXT
Titus 1:1, 4	Paul	Titus	Yes
Philemon 1–2	Paul	Philemon, et. al	Yes
Hebrews 13:22	Writer	Hebrew Christians	Yes
James 1:1	James	Twelve tribes	Yes
1 Peter 1:1	Peter	Asia Minor churches	Yes
2 Peter 1:1	Peter	Christians	Yes
1 John 2:1	John	John's friends	Yes
2 John 1	John, the Elder	the Chosen Lady	Yes
3 John 1	John, the Elder	Gaius	Yes
Jude 1	Jude	Christian friends	Yes

THE LOOK OF LETTERS IN THE FIRST CENTURY

Stylistically, Roman letters were rather loose, but they nearly always followed the same format.[5]

In the *greeting,* the sender would place his or her name first, followed by the person to whom the letter was sent, and then personal greetings. A typical salutation might have been: "Claudia Severa to her Lepidina, Greetings…" The *farewell* often restated the good wishes of the salutation, for example, "I pray that you are enjoying the best of fortune and are in good health."

Frequently the writer would use the services of an *amanuensis*—a secretary or scribe.

If the epistles in the New Testament are what they claim to be, we could expect that they would follow the usual practices for letter writing in the first century, and they do. Let's use Paul's letters to compare the New Testament letter with what we know is typical of letters in the Roman world.

1. SENDER'S NAME. Look at any one of the recognized thirteen Pauline epistles, and you will notice that they all begin with the same word—*Paul*. That's because Paul identifies himself as the sender in each of his letters, just as you would expect in the first century. It's a form he never varied because it's the form he learned in school as a boy living under the Roman Empire.[6]

2. RECIPIENT'S NAME. Next look at verse 1 and verse 2 (or, in the case of Romans, verse 7) of each of Paul's epistles. There you'll find the recipients' names. He writes to "the church of God in Corinth," or to "all the saints in Christ Jesus who are in Philippi," or to "Timothy, a true son in the faith." Each time the recipient is clear, just like in other letters of the Roman Empire.

3. GREETINGS (SALUTATION). In the place of the general word *greetings*, the apostle includes a special spiritual greeting of "grace and peace."[7] You'll find this in one of the first three verses of every letter except Titus, where it is in verse 4, and Romans, where it is in verse 7. "Grace and peace" seem to be Paul's way of uniting the Greek and Jewish factions of the early church. He was the "bridge" between the two parties in the church. *Grace* is the Greek greeting *charis,* and *peace* is the classic Hebrew greeting *shalom.* To both Jews and Gentiles reading his letters, Paul was saying, "Grace and shalom, y'all."

4. FAREWELL. The farewell in Paul's epistles is quite varied. Romans ends with a doxology (16:25–27). First Corinthians ends with a wish of grace to all and a reminder of Paul's love (16:23–24). The farewell of 2 Corinthians is especially touching (13:11–14). Ephesians ends with a

string of power words—peace, love, faith, grace (6:23–24). The reminder to greet one another with a wholesome kiss is part of the farewell in four of Paul's letters (Romans 16:16; 1 Corinthians 16:20; 2 Corinthians 13:12; 1 Thessalonians 5:26). Colossians ends with a sad reminder of Paul's imprisonment (4:18).

5. AMANUENSIS. The use of a scribe is frequently seen in the Old Testament.[8] That practice continued in the New Testament. In fact, in Romans 16:22, Paul's amanuensis identified himself as Tertius. To the Galatians, Paul says, "See what large letters I use as I write to you with my own hand!" (6:11). This may indicate that Paul was so upset with the spiritual immaturity of the Galatian churches that, rather than use a secretary, he wrote the letter himself.

6. SIGNATURE. Paul liked to sign his letters. Near the end of 1 Corinthians, Paul attests, "I, Paul, write this greeting in my own hand" (16:21). In the last verse of Colossians, Paul mentions, "I, Paul, write this greeting in my own hand" (4:18). At the conclusion of 2 Thessalonians, the apostle writes, "I, Paul, write this greeting in my own hand, which is the distinguishing mark in all my letters. This is how I write" (3:17). Perhaps he felt that his signature gave added authenticity to his letters or made them more personal.

We find the same parallels in the epistles of Peter, James, John, and Jude. These were genuine letters written by verifiable people of the first century.

The Letter from God's
Heart to Yours

Knowing that the Bible follows the typical literary forms of its day may encourage you to read it, but when you read it, you'll discover that the message of the Bible is anything but typical. No other book bears such an important message. Jesus said, "You diligently study the Scriptures because you think that by them you possess eternal life" (John 5:39).

Unlike the famous writings of Hammurabi, Aristotle, or Thucydides, the words of the Bible did not have their origin in the minds of men, but in the mind of God: "Men spoke from God as they were carried along by the Holy Spirit" (2 Peter 1:21). The Bible may have been in the typical style of literature of its time, but it is anything but typical in origin. "All Scripture is God-breathed" (2 Timothy 3:16), a claim that cannot be seriously made by any other literary work in history.

God chose to use the style of writing in Bible times to communicate truth that would transcend Bible times. It is precious truth, important truth, eternal truth.

While the Bible contains more than fifty authentic ancient letters, here's the most important fact I'll present in this chapter—the Bible is itself an authentic letter, sent from the heart of God to people like you and me.

When my wife and I were dating, and I was away at college, we were separated by about three hundred miles. Since we didn't see each other very often, we wrote letters.

Looking back at those years now, I don't regret not having the immediacy of instant messaging or voice mail. We have something instantaneous communication doesn't give—

a permanent written record. My wife has a whole shoebox full of love letters that will go with her to her grave.

My letters to Linda were not perfumed, penned with a calligrapher's skill, or especially eloquent. But each one was from my heart and written with only her in mind—and that made all the difference to her.

God's love letter to you is a lot like that. It reveals His heart to you, and it tells you how special you are to the Creator of the universe.

God was wearing His feelings on His sleeve when He said to Israel, "I have loved you with an everlasting love; I have drawn you with lovingkindness" (Jeremiah 31:3). Jesus revealed His innermost heartache when He said, "O Jerusalem, Jerusalem, you who kill the prophets and stone those sent to you, how often I have longed to gather your children together, as a hen gathers her chicks under her wings, but you were not willing!" (Luke 13:34).

Think about it: The communication you and I need most from God is exactly what we have received from Him in His Word. We can embrace it with confidence. We can feel His heart expressed there. And through its amazing message, we can connect personally with Him.

12

THE BIBLE IS ABOUT JESUS CHRIST

The Bible is the prism by which the light of Jesus Christ is broken into its many beautiful colors.
—JOHN R. STOTT

IN THIS CHAPTER...

...identify Jesus Christ in every book of the Bible.

...trace the scarlet thread through the entire Bible.

...see how Jesus can bring you into God's presence.

When you watch a movie or read a novel, you want to know what it's about. Who is the central character? What is the most important message?

In the Bible, the answer to all the questions is one person—Jesus. Once you know this and follow the thread of His story from the first page to last, the whole reading experience makes more sense.

The central person of the Bible is Jesus of Nazareth, Son of God, Savior of the world. As I'll show you, His story is the "scarlet thread" of redemption that runs throughout Scripture. If you want to connect with God through His Word, you have to connect with Jesus in all the Scriptures.

He's there, on page 1. Jesus is the Creator God, the Person of the Godhead who actually performed creation (John 1:1–3; Colossians 1:15–16; Hebrews 1:1–2). He was there at the fall of mankind as the promise of a Redeemer (Genesis 3:15). His person is woven throughout the Old Testament in prophecy (Micah 5:2; Isaiah 7:14; 9:6; Isaiah 53).

He bursts onto the first page of the New Testament, where His genealogy shows Him to be a descendant of the patriarch Abraham and in the line of King David (Matthew 1:1–17). He is there as the central figure at Calvary. And He is there on the last page of the Bible: "The Alpha and the Omega, the First and the Last, the Beginning and the End" (Revelation 22:13). The final prayer of the Bible breathes His name: "Come, Lord Jesus" (22:20).

The key to discovering God in the Bible is to discover Jesus.

CHRIST IN THE PAGES OF THE BIBLE

Many authors have compiled their own lists of how you find Jesus Christ in each book of the Bible. I hope the following list I have developed will help you discover the one central Person in all the Scriptures.

CHRIST, THE CENTRAL PERSON IN THE BIBLE	
Genesis	Seed of Abraham (22:18)
Exodus	Passover Lamb (12:3–8, 12–13)
Leviticus	Great High Priest (21:10–12)
Numbers	Star of Jacob (24:17)

Deuteronomy	Prophet like Moses (34:10–12)
Joshua	Commander of the Lord's Army (4:14–15)
Judges	Messenger of Jehovah (13:8–10, 17–21)
Ruth	Kinsman-Redeemer (4:14)
1 Samuel	Man After God's Own Heart (13:14)
2 Samuel	Seed of David (7:12–13)
1 Kings	Still, Small Voice of God (19:12, NKJV)
2 Kings	King of Kings (23:25)
1 Chronicles	One Who Searches Our Hearts (28:9)
2 Chronicles	God Who Will Dwell on Earth (6:18)
Ezra	Lord of Heaven and Earth (5:11)
Nehemiah	Joy of the Lord (8:10)
Esther	God Above Time (4:14)
Job	Our Risen Redeemer (19:25–27)
Psalms	Our Shepherd (23:1); Our Secret Place (91:1)
Proverbs	Wisdom of God (4:5–8)
Ecclesiastes	One Who Makes All Things Beautiful (3:11)
Song of Solomon	Rose of Sharon and the Lily of the Valley (2:1)
Isaiah	Suffering Servant (53:2–7)
Jeremiah	The Lord Our Righteousness (23:6)
Lamentations	The God of Faithfulness (3:22–23)
Ezekiel	Coming Prince (44:1–3)
Daniel	Fourth Man in the Fire (3:25)
Hosea	Lover of Those Who Go Astray (14:4)
Joel	Outpourer of the Spirit (2:28)
Amos	Living Word of God (8:11)
Obadiah	Lord of His Kingdom (v. 21)
Jonah	God of the Second Chance (3:1)
Micah	The Bethlehemite (5:2)
Nahum	One Who Brings Good News (1:15)
Habakkuk	Lord in His Holy Temple (2:20)

Zephaniah	Lord in Israel's Midst (3:15)
Haggai	Desire of All Nations (2:7)
Zechariah	Branch (6:12); Coming King (9:9)
Malachi	Sun of Righteousness (4:2)
Matthew	King of the Jews (2:2; 27:11)
Mark	Servant of the Lord (10:43–45)
Luke	Son of Man (19:10)
John	Son of God (19:7)
Acts	The Ascended Lord (1:9–11)
Romans	The Lord Our Righteousness (10:4)
1 Corinthians	Firstfruits of the Dead (15:20)
2 Corinthians	Our Sufficiency (3:5, NKJV)
Galatians	Our Freedom (5:1)
Ephesians	Head of the Church (5:23)
Philippians	Highly Exalted Lord (2:9)
Colossians	Fullness of the Godhead (2:9, NKJV)
1 Thessalonians	The Coming Lord (4:16–17)
2 Thessalonians	The Coming Lord (1:7–8)
1 Timothy	Mediator Between God and Man (2:5)
2 Timothy	One Who Stands by Our Side (4:17)
Titus	Our Great God and Savior (2:13)
Philemon	The One Who Paid Our Debt (v. 18)
Hebrews	Great High Priest (4:14)
James	Lord Drawing Near (4:8)
1 Peter	The Suffering Lamb (1:19)
2 Peter	Lord of Glory (1:16–17)
1 John	Coming Son of God (2:28)
2 John	Son of God and Son of Man (v. 7)
3 John	The Truth (vv. 3–4)
Jude	Coming Judge (vv. 14–15)
Revelation	The Lord's Christ (11:15)

No matter where you look in the Bible, Jesus is there.[1] To miss Jesus in the Bible is like missing George Bailey in *It's a Wonderful Life* or the count in *The Count of Monte Cristo*. If you miss the main character, you miss everything!

FOLLOWING THE SCARLET THREAD

Everything about the central character in the Bible points to a central, dramatic event—His sacrifice at Calvary. Everything in the Old Testament points forward to Calvary; everything in the Gospels relates Jesus' life to that event; and everything in the rest of the New Testament points back to it.

The death, burial, and resurrection of Jesus are the crux of history.

The idea of the scarlet thread originates with the story of Rahab, the prostitute of Jericho. The two spies Joshua sent on a reconnaissance mission to check out the strength of Jericho's fortification stayed at Rahab's inn. The woman said, "I know that the LORD has given this land to you and that a great fear of you has fallen on us...for the LORD your God is God in heaven above and on the earth below" (Joshua 2:9, 11). She asked the men to spare her and her family when they returned with their army of Israel. In order to identify that she was under the protection of the Most High God, she tied a scarlet cord in the window, a blood-red sign of salvation.

This thread of redemption shows up often throughout the Bible and has been noticed by many scholars. Matthew Henry described it this way, "A golden thread of gospel grace runs through the whole web of the Old Testament"[2] W. A. Criswell once preached a watch night service on New Year's Eve from

7:30 P.M. until past midnight. His theme for this marathon message was "The Scarlet Thread Through the Bible." It was later published as a book.[3]

Let's do some tracking of our own in the Bible to uncover that scarlet thread.

1. BLOOD IN THE GARDEN. After Adam and Eve sinned in the Garden, they tried to cover themselves with fig leaves. But the real problem ran too deep for that. There, as at the cross, God provided the answer for them. He took an innocent animal, and as Adam and Eve watched, He sacrificed the animal, then made coats of skin for our first parents (Genesis 3:1–13, 21). This was the first sacrifice in the Bible. There would be many more because God always requires a blood sacrifice in payment for our sin.

2. BLOOD ON THE HEEL. In the midst of severe consequences that came from the first sin, God made a promise of hope. He said to the serpent, "And I will put enmity between you and the woman, and between your offspring [seed] and hers; he will crush your head, and you will strike his heel" (Genesis 3:15). We know from the Gospels that Satan struck a bloody blow to the heel of the Savior at the cross. But it was not a permanent blow. Jesus triumphed at the Resurrection and will ultimately crush the head of that old snake Satan (Revelation 20:7–10).

3. BLOOD ON A BROTHER. After a while, Adam and Eve gave birth to sons Cain and Abel (Genesis 4:1–10). Cain pridefully brought to God the firstfruits of the field, but he did

it "like a displayer at a country fair."[4] His brother Abel brought the first lamb of his flock and offered it to God humbly, a preview of Christ's offering at Calvary. God respected Abel's blood sacrifice because it was from his heart and was offered in faith (Hebrews 11:4). But He showed contempt for Cain's proud offering.

4. BLOOD ON THE ALTAR. In the time of Noah, humanity's terrible wickedness brought the cataclysmic judgment of the Flood. After the waters receded, the Bible says:

> Noah built an altar to the LORD and, taking some of all the clean animals and clean birds, he sacrificed burnt offerings on it. The LORD smelled the pleasing aroma and said in his heart: "Never again will I curse the ground because of man, even though every inclination of his heart is evil from childhood." (Genesis 8:20–22)

5. BLOOD ON THE DOOR. After God had identified Abraham as the Father of His chosen people, the Jews, his descendants became slaves to the Egyptians. But God called Moses to be their deliverer. In a mighty struggle between God and Pharaoh, God told Moses that He would bring a plague of death on the firstborn of the Egyptians. For Israel to escape, they would have to paint their doorposts with the blood of a lamb: "The blood will be a sign for you on the houses where you are; and when I see the blood, I will pass over you" (Exodus 12:13).

Similarly, the only way for you and me to avoid judgment for our sins is to apply the blood of Jesus, the Lamb of God (John 1:29), to our lives. Jesus bled and died that we might have eternal life.

THE ULTIMATE SACRIFICE, THE ULTIMATE INVITATION

Let's fast-forward to the New Testament. What was foreshadowed in the Old Testament played out in the New Testament on the stage of Jesus' life. When Jesus launched His ministry at age thirty, John the Baptist introduced Him by announcing, "Look, the Lamb of God, who takes away the sin of the world" (John 1:29).

What a revolutionary concept—not repeated sacrifices to remove the penalty of individual sins, but the Lamb of God, sacrificed *once* to forever remove the penalty of sin for the entire world!

When Jesus was crucified between two thieves, He shouted a great cry of victory: "It is finished" (John 19:30). The Lamb of God had been slain. The atonement for sin was made. The salvation of sinful people was now possible.

One of the soldiers "pierced Jesus' side with a spear, bringing a sudden flow of blood and water" (John 19:34). The blood of the Lamb was spilled. Everything that the scarlet thread led to was now accomplished. Then, at the very moment Jesus died, the curtain of the temple was torn in two from top to bottom. The veil that had kept people from the intimate presence of God was ripped apart.

Do you see now how that scarlet thread leads to the life-changing connection we have been studying? It's as if after Christ's death at Calvary, God said, "Through the blood of Jesus, you now have access to Me anytime, day or night."

"For you know that it was not with perishable things such as silver or gold that you were redeemed," Peter wrote to early Christians, "…but with the precious blood of Christ, a lamb without blemish or defect" (1 Peter 1:18–19).

Who can bring you into the very presence of the God of the Bible? It is none other than the central Person of the Bible—Jesus Christ, the Lamb of God. He is the centerpiece of God's plan of salvation.

13

THE BIBLE IS ACCESSIBLE TO EVERYONE

Bible reading is an education in itself.
—ALFRED LORD TENNYSON

IN THIS CHAPTER...

...learn how easy it is to read God's Word.

...uncover how much time it takes to read the books of the Bible.

...discover how to maximize your time in the Word.

Michael Billester was a Bible distributor in Poland just before World War II. One day he entered a tiny village and gave a man a Bible. The man promised to read it, and he did. He discovered that God loved him and sent His Son to die for him. The man did what the Philippian jailer did (Acts 16:31): He trusted Jesus Christ as Savior. After he read the Bible through, the Polish man gave it to others in the little village so they could read it. This was the only copy of the Bible in the whole village, but from that one Bible, two hundred people came to faith in Christ.

After the war was over, Billester returned to the village to preach. He was amazed that so many people had been converted because of that one Bible. They flocked to hear him speak. So impressed was Billester that he asked everybody in the audience to quote their favorite verse of Scripture before he spoke. One puzzled man hesitantly stood and questioned, "Perhaps we didn't understand. Did you mean quote our favorite verse or our favorite chapter of the Bible?"

In this final chapter I want to challenge you to get the most from the treasure of your Bible every time you pick it up.

If you'll do what those Polish villagers did—open the Bible, read it, and own it for yourself—you'll meet God in new and powerful ways.

UNOPENED TREASURE

Some people believe that reading the Bible is difficult, or so they've been told. But that's not true. Yes, the Ethiopian eunuch in Acts 8 was having difficulty understanding what he read in God's Word. When Philip asked, "Do you understand what you are reading?" the Ethiopian answered, "How can I, unless someone explains it to me?" (vv. 30–31). So Philip began where the man was reading and told him the good news about Jesus.

But the Ethiopian eunuch didn't have all the advantages for understanding the Bible that you have. He was an Ethiopian reading Hebrew. There was a language barrier. You have none. He was without a teacher, commentaries, books, tapes, videos, seminars, on-line resources, CD-ROM, etc. You have a plethora of aids to help with your understanding. He was alone, with no church, no pastor, no mentor, no small group leader—no one. You have many, if not all, of these resources.

Most important, the Ethiopian did not have the benefit of the Holy Spirit. But Christians have both the presence of the Spirit and the power of His teaching to help us know God more intimately (John 14:16–18, 26). You've got a lot going for you to help you understand the Bible. But to understand it, one thing is certain...

You've got to read it!

The Bible is the all-time bestselling book—the one that people cherish and rush to when they need comfort. So you would expect this book, more than any other, to be read and reread regularly. But as a growing body of evidence attests, the Bible is *the best-loved, least-read book of all time.*

The observation of pollster George Gallup Jr. seems to be right on target: "Americans revere the Bible—but, by and large, they don't read it. And because they don't read it, they have become a nation of biblical illiterates."[1]

As a part of his "Annual Survey of America's Faith," George Barna reported near the close of the twentieth century that the percentage of people who had read their Bible "in the past seven days" was 36 percent. That may not sound too bad, except that the number was 45 percent near the beginning of the decade.[2] I have often said that if Christians blew the dust off their Bibles at the same time, we'd all get killed in the dust storm.

If you are to benefit from God's Word, you're going to have to read it. It's how you connect with God.

OLD MYTHS, NEW FACTS

Even those Christians who do read their Bibles apparently aren't reading them too closely. Barna observed, "Nine out of ten adults own a Bible. Most adults read the Bible during the year and a huge majority claims they know all of the basic teachings of the Bible." He then asks, "How, then, can most people say Satan does not exist, that the Holy Spirit is merely a symbol, that eternal peace with God can be earned through good works?" Barna laments, "In a sound bite society you get sound bite theology."[3]

If we all have Bibles in our own language and a translation we can understand and appreciate, why don't we read the Bible more? Some say the Bible doesn't have anything to say to them. Others admit that they don't read the Bible because it doesn't confirm what they already believe. Many people—maybe you're one of them—feel that reading the Bible just requires too much of a time commitment. But are you sure?

Did you know that half of the books of the Bible can be read in less time than it takes you to watch the evening news? Half of them! Suppose you wanted to read all the way through the Bible—Genesis to Revelation. How long would it take? A week? A month? A year? Actually, *you can read the entire Bible in less than seventy-two hours*. Not as much time as you thought, is it?

Here are some facts you should know about reading the Bible:

- Forty books of the Bible can be read in an hour or less.
- Thirty-three of the sixty-six books of the Bible can be read in less than thirty minutes.

- Twenty-six books of the Bible can be read in less than fifteen minutes.

Are you surprised? Wait…there's more.[4]

- Eleven books of the Old Testament can be read in fifteen minutes or less.
- Fifteen books in the New Testament can be read in fifteen minutes or less.
- One book in the Old Testament and four in the New have only one chapter.
- Fifteen books of the Old Testament contain ten or fewer chapters.
- Only four books of the Old Testament have more than fifty chapters.
- Seventeen books of the New Testament contain less than ten chapters.
- Only two books of the New Testament contain more than twenty-five chapters.
- Second John and 3 John can be read in about two minutes each.
- While the first book of the Bible may take more than three hours to read, the last one takes only about an hour.

Becoming intimate with God, however, is not a speed-reading contest. It takes time and thought. Still, the old excuse we use that it takes too long to read the Bible seems to be no more true than today's other urban legends.

A PLAN FOR TREASURING
GOD'S WORDS

The longest psalm in the Bible, written by a devout but unnamed psalmist, gives us an inside view of how a person thinks, feels, and lives if he or she really treasures God's words. Almost every verse in Psalm 119 has something to say about the Scripture.[5] The psalmist used a variety of synonyms when referring to God's Word, like *statutes*, *ordinances*, *testimonies*, *commandments*, *precepts*, and more. You can't read this psalm and not be impressed with the author's deep love and respect for God's Word.

Put your finger on just about any verse in Psalm 119, and you're going to get help finding God in His Word. But since this is the longest of the psalms, let's limit our advice-seeking to the "Beth" section, verses 9–16. What does the psalmist have to tell us here about maximizing our time with God? I see nine specifics:

1. Heed

In verse 9, we see the classic answer to the question of how a young man can keep his way pure: "By taking heed thereto according to thy word" (KJV). To *heed* means to "keep" or "guard" what God says and let it play out in your everyday life. It means to be very careful to live the words of Scripture. This concept is so important that it was repeated in twenty-one verses of Psalm 119.[6] You maximize your time in God's Word when you put into practice what you read.

Joshua 1:8 describes both the commitment to living the words of God and its wonderful consequences: "Do not let this Book of the Law depart from your mouth; meditate on it day and night, so that you may be careful to do everything written in it. Then you will be prosperous and successful."

Only when you take special care to practice in life what you read in God's Word will you have truly benefited from reading the Bible.

2. Save

When I was a kid growing up, there wasn't much talk of building up personal cash reserves. My father and mother just tried to keep enough food on the table to feed us hungry boys. These days, talk of 401(k)s, IRAs, and certificates of deposit is common around company break rooms.

"Storing up" is what the psalmist meant when he said, "I have hidden your word in my heart" (v. 11). He had spent many hours as a young shepherd tucking away God's Word in his heart. When he needed the strength that only God could provide, what he had stored up came spilling out.

Martin and Gracia Burnham were held hostage for over a year by the Abu Sayyaf guerillas in the Philippines. Eventually, a gun battle freed Gracia but took Martin's life. I interviewed Gracia Burnham on several *Back to the Bible* programs shortly after her release. "Martin and I would quote Scripture together that we had learned," Gracia said. "He would always encourage me with the words from the Bible."

You may never face terror like the Burnhams faced, but when you memorize Scripture, it's like making a deposit in the bank. That deposit builds with interest, and when you need it, your deposit is there. And it's FDIC insured: "Forever Dependable In Christ."

3. Repeat

I have vivid memories of my children learning math for the first time. They breezed through simple addition, but multiplication and division were more difficult. The only way they could get those multiplication tables down pat was through repetition.

Meaningful repetition of Bible verses, Bible truths, Bible promises, and Bible principles is not quite like learning multiplication tables, but as teachers will tell you, repetition is a key to learning. The author of Psalm 119 was familiar with the concept, because when he said, "O LORD; teach me your decrees" (v. 12), he used the common word for describing how a teacher drilled a class until they had mastered the material.[7]

When you learn something new from your Bible, write it down in a journal, a spiral-bound notebook, or on your laptop or handheld—wherever you record important things. Tomorrow when you sneak away for some quiet time with God, go back and repeat what you noted yesterday. A week later do the same thing. A month later repeat it again. Repeat it as often as it takes to make that truth a part of you.

4. Share

The author of Psalm 119 was the learner in verse 12. But the learner became the teacher in verse 13. He wrote, "With my lips I recount all the laws that come from your mouth."

One of the best ways to make something permanent in your mind and heart is to be vocal about it. Talk it up. Share what you've learned with others. I used to think to myself, *My friends probably discovered this a long time ago. They'll think I'm a little slow if I share what I've learned with them.* But when I tried it, more often than not it was a new insight to them as well.

When the psalmist wrote, "I *recount* all the laws that come from your mouth," he used a word that means "to enumerate." In other words, when you learn something from the Bible, share everything you have learned with your friends. Enumerate what you discover and it will be not only yours, but theirs as well.

In 1919, a man recovering from injuries sustained during World War I rented a small apartment in Chicago. He chose the apartment because of its proximity to Sherwood Anderson, the famous author who had written the novel *Winesburg, Ohio.* Anderson was known for his willingness to help young writers. Over shared meals, the men discussed writing and Anderson gave brutal critiques of the younger man's work. In 1926 the young protégé published his first novel, *The Sun Also Rises.* His name was Ernest Hemingway.

After Hemingway left Chicago, Anderson moved to New Orleans. He met another young wordsmith and critiqued his writing. He helped him develop a character and a story for his novel *The Sound and the Fury.* This man was William Faulkner. Later, in California, Anderson mentored playwright Thomas Wolfe and novelist John Steinbeck.

Three of Anderson's young charges won Nobel Prizes, and all four won Pulitzer Prizes. Why did Anderson give so much of himself? Because he also sat under the influence of a mentor, the great Carl Sandburg.

When you pass on what you've learned from God's Word, its power is amplified in your own life. And you will impact others in ways that will change lives…and maybe even history.

5. Rejoice

If you want to get the most from your time in the Word, practice joy in what you read—all of it. The psalmist wrote, "I rejoice in following your statutes as one rejoices in great riches" (v. 14).

Of course, some Bible truths—God loves you and God will never leave you, for example—are easy to rejoice in. Other truths—God is a holy judge, or God sees everything you do—may not be so easy. But even though you won't like everything you read in the Bible, all of God's truth is meant for your well-being.

To rejoice in a warning or a difficult teaching is an act of faith that honors God. But it also opens the door for personal change in your life. I'm reminded of a story that Pastor Samuel Naftal of Mozambique tells, about how mosquitoes saved his life. During severe flooding, Naftal and sixteen others clung to tree limbs for almost two days. Naftal used the time to preach to those around him. But eventually exhaustion set in. Then mosquitoes began to swarm around everyone, biting them unmercifully. According to Naftal, it was those bites that kept the refugees from dozing off and falling from their perches into the raging waters!

Sometimes God's most important truths for us are the ones we *least* want to hear. But as we receive His Word—all of it—and find our happiness in it, we will receive His fullest blessings.

6. Muse

As I wrote in chapter 3, if you and I fail to ponder what God says, we are likely to fail to remember it. The psalmist under-

stood the value of mental musing: "I meditate on your precepts and consider your ways" (v. 15). By "meditate," he meant
take the time to reflect over what you read, engaging in some
creative discussion about it with yourself. The psalmist Asaph
suggested the same when he wrote: "I remembered my songs
in the night. My heart mused and my spirit inquired" (77:6).

Allowing God's Word to seep into every corner of your
mind takes a time commitment that not all are willing to
make. But it may be the most valuable commitment you make
today. Take a lesson from jungle dwellers: A big-game hunter
traveling deep into Africa's jungle hired natives to carry his
loads. The first day the hunter really pushed his entourage as
they made their way deep into the jungle. The man had high
hopes of getting to his hunting destination quickly. But on the
second morning his carriers refused to move. They com-
plained that the day before they had gone too fast and were
now waiting for their souls to catch up with their bodies.

Musing over God's Word gives your soul time to catch up
with your body, and that may be one of the missing ingredi-
ents in connecting with God.

7. Consider

It's easy to read without paying attention to what we're reading. That's why the author of Psalm 119 told God he would
be careful to "consider your ways" (v. 15). The word *consider*
means to deliberate and evaluate diligently—to mentally look
at what you're reading from many perspectives.

When Samuel was to select the king of Israel from Jesse's
sons, he was counseled by God, "Do not consider his appearance or his height, for I have rejected him. The LORD does not

look at the things man looks at. Man looks at the outward appearance, but the LORD looks at the heart" (1 Samuel 16:7). In the same way, we can turn the truths of God's Word over in our mind throughout the day, looking for new insights and new ways to apply them to our choices.

8. Cherish

The psalmist genuinely loved his Bible. Verse 16 says, "I delight in your decrees." *Delight* is a very tender and expressive word, isn't it? In the Hebrew, it means "to stroke" or "to fondle." It's what you do when you bring a baby home from the hospital. You are gentle and loving as you express your delight in your newborn.

In Isaiah 66:12, God speaks of a future day when Israel will come back to Him and says, "I will extend peace to her like a river, and the wealth of nations like a flooding stream; you will nurse and be carried on her arm and dandled on her knees." I like that expression, "dandled on her knees." *Webster's* defines *dandle* as "to move [as a baby] up and down in one's arms or on one's knee in affectionate play."[8]

That's the way the psalmist feels about God's Word. He cherishes its wonders and its life-giving insights—and cherishes even more what they reveal about its Author.

9. Remember

Think about the things you forget. You forget your keys. You forget your anniversary. You forget your kid's birthday. You forget what you went into another room to get…

If you want to connect with God's heart, the one thing you don't want to forget is His Word. Verse 16 says, "I delight in your decrees; I will not neglect your word." Our mentor in Psalm 119 refused to ignore the Word of God through benign neglect. He would not allow a day to go by without becoming more intimate with His heavenly Father.

Our opportunity, then, is to keep God's Word in our thoughts, on our tongues, by our bedside, in our offices and kitchens, and as a natural part of our relationships. Good things *do* get forgotten, or at least marginalized. Let's makes sure that the precious words of God—and an awareness of His presence—are at the very center of our daily lives.

THE BEST THING IN LIFE

Her mother was startled to find seven-year-old Karen going through her new Bible and circling the word *God* everywhere she found it. When her mother asked why she was doing that, Karen replied, "So I'll know where to find God when I need Him."

When you need God, and at any other time in life, the best place to find Him is where He reveals Himself—in His Word. The Bible is a revelation of God—His person, His character, His purposes. When you read your Bible to find God rather than to discover principles to guide your life, an amazing thing happens.

You find both.

EPILOGUE

We slander God by our eagerness to
serve God without knowing Him.

—J. OSWALD CHAMBERS

Connect \ke-ˈnekt\ *verb:*
to become joined;
to establish a rapport;
to establish a relationship.

God has done all that is necessary for us to establish a rapport
with Him. He did not leave us to guess at His will, His plans,
or His goals for us. He gave us His Word, detailing all we need
in order to establish an intimate relationship with Him. Now
He waits for you and me to read the Word, discover the joys
of being joined to Him, and progress on our quest to connect
with God.

C. S. Lewis was amazed at the psalmists' longing to *know*.

He wrote:

> These poets knew far less reason than we for loving God. They did not know that He offered them eternal joy; still less that He would die to win it for them. Yet they express a longing for Him, for His mere presence, which comes only to the best Christians or to Christians in their best moments.[1]

I often wonder if we Christians, with all our enlightenment through the Gospels and epistles, have lost the wonder these simple psalmists had of connecting with God. Have we replaced wonder with ignorance? Or even knowledge? Are we taking a step further away from God by replacing knowledge with feelings?

It's time for you to put this book down and pick up one much greater—God's book, the Bible. In reading it, you will connect with God's heart.

Intimacy with God comes through attachment to Him, and attachment comes through contact. To connect with God's heart, read His Word and then follow the advice of Mary, the mother of Jesus: "Do whatever he tells you" (John 2:5). When you do, you'll connect with God in ways you never thought possible.

NOTES

Preface

1. Though people today are on a spiritual quest, many of them are not on a quest for God. They presume to find their spirituality elsewhere. George Barna notes, "Desiring to have a close, personal relationship with God ranks just sixth among the 21 life goals tested, trailing such desires as 'living a comfortable lifestyle.'" George Barna, "The Year's Most Intriguing Findings, From Barna Research Studies," *Barna Research Online*, December 12, 2000. http://www.barna.org/cgi-bin/PagePress Release.asp?PressReleaseID=77&Reference=B (accessed 10 December 2003).
2. Jim Cymbala, *The Life God Blesses* (Grand Rapids, MI: Zondervan, 2001), 9.
3. A. W. Tozer, *The Pursuit of God* (Camp Hill, PA: Christian Publications, Inc., 1982), 11.

Chapter One

1. While *The Matrix* grossed $170 million in the United States, another $460 million worldwide, and influenced numerous movies, computer games, and commercials, it is nonetheless an R-rated film and is not recommended for Christian viewers. It was the first DVD to sell more than 1 million copies.

2. The following passages refer to God speaking to Moses: Exodus 3:7; 4:2, 4, 6, 11, 19, 21; 6:1, 26; 7:1, 14; 8:16, 20; 9:1, 8, 13, 22; 10:12, 21; 11:1, 9; 12:43; 14:15, 26; 17:5, 14; 19:9–10, 21, 24; 20:22; 24:12; 30:34; 32:7, 9, 27, 33; 33:1, 17, 21; 34:1, 27; Leviticus 16:2; 21:1; Numbers 3:40; 7:11; 11:16, 23; 12:14; 14:11, 20; 15:35; 16:40; 17:10; 21:8, 34; 25:4; 27:12, 18; Deuteronomy 1:42; 2:9, 31; 3:2, 26; 4:10; 5:28; 9:12; 10:1, 11; 18:17; 31:14, 16; 34:4; Joshua 11:23; 14:6.

Chapter Two

1. Woodrow M. Kroll, *Early in the Morning: Devotionals for Early Risers* (Neptune, NJ: Loizeaux, 1994), 213.
2. Here's a partial list of Bible versions popular today: King James Version (KJV, also known as the Authorized Version); New King James Version (NKJV); New International Version (NIV); New American Standard Bible (NASB); New Living Translation (NLT); Contemporary English Version (CEV); English Standard Version (ESV); New Revised Standard Version (NRSV); and *The Message*.
3. The most widely used exhaustive concordance today is *Strong's Exhaustive Concordance of the Bible* by James Strong. *Cruden's Complete Concordance* and *Young's Analytical Concordance* are still available, although not as popular. Also available are revisions and expansions of Strong's: *The New Strong's Exhaustive Concordance, Expanded,* and *The Strongest Strong's Exhaustive Concordance, 21st Century Edition*. Most of these are based

on the KJV text. For concordances of other versions see: *Zondervan NIV Exhaustive Concordance; Zondervan NASB Exhaustive Concordance; The Complete Concordance to the Bible New King James Version*; and *The Concise Concordance to the NRSV*.

4. For example, QuickVerse, PC Study Bible, Logos, Online Bible, Bibleworks, and MyBible (palm pilot).

5. Popular Bible dictionaries include: *Nelson's Illustrated Bible Dictionary, Nelson's New Illustrated Bible Dictionary, New International Bible Dictionary, Eerdman's Dictionary of the Bible, The New Unger's Bible Dictionary, New Bible Dictionary, Wycliffe Bible Dictionary, Zondervan Pictorial Bible Dictionary, HarperCollins Bible Dictionary*, and *Holman Bible Dictionary*.

6. Reliable Bible maps and/or Bible atlases include: *The Oxford Bible Atlas* (May), *Atlas of the Bible Lands* (Frank), and *The Moody Atlas of Bible Lands* (Beitzel).

7. Good one-volume commentaries include: *The King James Bible Commentary* (Hindson and Kroll); *Believer's Bible Commentary* (MacDonald); *The New International Bible Commentary* (Bruce); *Baker Commentary on the Bible* (Elwell); *The Wycliffe Bible Commentary* (Pfeiffer and Harrison); *New Bible Commentary, 21st Century Edition* (Wenham, Motyer, Carson, and France); and the *Chapter by Chapter Bible Commentary* (Wiersbe). Good two-volume Bible commentaries include: *Zondervan NIV Bible Commentary* (Barker and Kohlenberger); and *The IVP Bible Background Commentary* (Keener). A good three-volume commentary is *The Bible Knowledge*

Commentary (Walvoord, Zuck, and Bock). A good six-volume commentary is *The Bible Exposition Commentary* (Wiersbe).

8. Archibald Hart, *Adrenalin and Stress* (Dallas, TX: Word, 1991), 151.

Chapter Three

1. For the benefits of reading God's Word one entire book at a time, helpful hints on how to do so, and a guide to each book, see Woodrow Kroll, *Read Your Bible, One Book at a Time* (Ann Arbor, MI: Vine Books, 2002).

2. Elmer Towns, *A Beginner's Guide to Reading the Bible* (Ann Arbor, MI: Vine Books, 2001).

3. Asaph promised that the Jews would not hide God's Word from their children, but would verbally tell each generation what God commanded the fathers (Psalm 78:4–7). This is exactly what the fathers were told to do in Deuteronomy 6:3–7, but they began with the oral reading of God's Word. So important was reading the Scriptures aloud both in Old Testament and New Testament times that those who read silently, like the majority of Christians today, were deemed to be cheating themselves. Some educational psychologists today estimate that if you read out loud, you will retain what you read at a 200 to 300 percent greater capacity—reason enough to read the Bible aloud.

4. John Harries, *G. Campbell Morgan, The Man and His Ministry* (Old Tappan, NJ: Fleming Revell, 1930), 199.

5. A. W. Tozer, *The Pursuit of God* (Camp Hill, PA: Christian Publications, Inc., 1982), 69.

6. Quoted in John Piper, *Desiring God* (Portland, OR: Multnomah Press, 1986), 116.

Chapter Four

1. John Bunyan, *Grace Abounding to the Chief of Sinners* (Oxford: The Clarendon Press, 1962), 102.
2. Jeremiah 10:11; Daniel 2:4–7:28; and Ezra 4:8–6:18; 7:12–26. There are also several Aramaic words and phrases in the New Testament, such as *Talitha Koum* (Mark 5:41); *Ephphatha* (7:34); *Eloi, Eloi, lama sabachthani* (Matthew 27:46; Mark 15:34); *Maranatha* (1 Corinthians 16:22, KJV); *Abba*, Father (Mark 14:36; Romans 8:15; Galatians 4:6).
3. *Vine's Complete Expository Dictionary of Old and New Testament Words* (Vine, Unger & White, Jr.); *The Book Study Concordance of the Greek New Testament* (Kostenberger & Bouchoc); *Theological Wordbook of the Old Testament*, 2 Volumes (Harris, Archer, Jr. & Waltke); *Word Studies in the Greek New Testament*, 4 Volumes (Wuest); *Analytical Key to the Old Testament* (Owens), to name a few.

Chapter Five

1. "Jedi 'religion' grows in Australia," *BBC News World Edition*, August 27, 2002. http://news.bbc.co.uk/2/hi/entertainment/2218456.stm (accessed 19 December 2003). "The majority do not

seriously tell each other: 'May the force be with you,'
according to Australian Star Wars Appreciation Society
president Chris Brennan. When you look at it you
probably have got about 5,000 people in that 70,000
that were true hard-core people that would believe the
Jedi religion carte blanche," he told ABC Radio.
2. Nicholas of Cusa, *The Vision of God* (New York: E. P.
Dutton & Sons, 1928), 60.
3. Jim Elliot, "The Journals of Jim Elliot," *Christianity Today*,
16 January 1951.

Chapter Six

1. The "dust of the ground" should not be viewed as
pulverized earth but as the elements of the earth. Martin
Luther rendered the Hebrew with the German word
Erdenkloss, literally "lump of earth." This term does not
mean mud, but earth.
2. Groups of living organisms belong in the same created
"kind" if they have descended from the same ancestral
gene pool. This does not preclude the development of a
new species because that represents a partitioning of the
original gene pool. Biologically, a new variation could
arise within a species when a population is isolated and
inbreeding occurs. But this is not a new "kind," just a
further partitioning of an existing kind. We were not
created as divine, but were created in God's image and
therefore are closer to God in kind than we are to
animals. We are not of the same species—He is divine; we
are human—but we are of the same image and likeness.

3. Hebrew *demuwth*.

4. William Shakespeare, *Macbeth*, ed. Barbara A. Mowat, et al. (New York: Washington Square Press, 1992), 5.5.27–30.

Chapter Seven

1. Direct references to God's will for us are made in the following verses: Matthew 18:14; John 6:40; Ephesians 5:17–18; 1 Thessalonians 4:3–7; 5:16–18; 1 Peter 2:13–15; 3:15–17. Almost every book of the New Testament has something to say about God's will. Some examples are: Matthew 7:21; Acts 21:14; Romans 12:2; 2 Corinthians 8:5; Galatians 1:4; 1 Peter 4:2, 19; 1 John 2:17.

2. The word *image* means "exact representation," like the head of a king imprinted on a coin. Jesus is the Father's exact representation. If you want to see the Father, look at the Son.

3. The word *firstborn* means two things: (1) He preceded the whole of His creation; and (2) He is sovereign over all of His creation. *Firstborn* is the common Old Testament designation for the Messiah-God: "I will also appoint him my firstborn, the most exalted of the kings of the earth" (Psalm 89:27). Clearly the title indicates position, not generation. As the Creator God, Jesus not only preceded His creation (the Creator must precede the creation), but, as the Sovereign God, He is in a position over all His creation.

4. The Creator God of Genesis 1 is Jesus. While all persons of the Godhead participated in the creation in some way, it was God the Son who was charged with the actual act of creation (John 1:1–2, 14). "In the past God spoke to our forefathers through the prophets at many times and in various ways, but in these last days he has spoken to us by his Son, whom he appointed heir of all things, and through whom he made the universe" (Hebrews 1:1–2).

5. "And God placed all things under his feet and appointed him to be head over everything for the church, which is his body" (Ephesians 1:22–23).

6. Christ was the first to be resurrected with an immortal body (1 Corinthians 15:20). He says, "Because I live, you also will live" (John 14:19).

7. The word is *pleroma* in Greek and means that Jesus has all it takes to be God. "For in Christ all the fullness of the Deity lives in bodily form" (Colossians 2:9). Our finite minds may not be able to comprehend exactly everything necessary for God to be God, but we can understand this: All it takes, Jesus has.

8. "Therefore, since we have been justified through faith, we have peace with God through our Lord Jesus Christ" (Romans 5:1).

9. Gertrude Himmelfarb, *The DeMoralizing of Society* (New York: Alfred A. Knopf, 1994), 11.

10. The Greek prefix *hupo* means "under," and the verb *tasso* means "to arrange." In each case in this passage, the word translated *submit* is *hupotasso*.

Chapter Eight

1. The word Paul uses for *overflowing* is *perisseuo* in Greek. It means to exceed, or be more than abundant. Paul used it in 1 Corinthians 15:58 when he said, "Therefore, my beloved brethren, be steadfast, immovable, always abounding in the work of the Lord, knowing that your labor is not in vain in the Lord" (NKJV).

2. For true stories of hope that will lift your spirits and encourage your heart, read *Hope Grows In Winter* by Woodrow Kroll and George Miller III (Kregel Books). In each chapter someone who faced disaster of difficulty tells their own story of how they discovered God in His Word and as a result discovered hope.

3. "Proud to Be American, Even with the Jitters," *USA Today Online*, 11 October 2001.

Chapter Nine

1. See William Bennett, *The De-Valuing of America* (Colorado Springs, CO: Focus on the Family Publishing, 1994).

2. James D. Hunter, *Culture Wars: The Struggle to Define America* (New York: Basic Books, 1991).

3. Bishop Gene Robinson is a founding member of Concord Outright, a support group for gay/lesbian and questioning teens. At this date, he is the only openly gay bishop of the Episcopal church. Susan Candiotti, "Gay Episcopal bishop candidate receives panel's OK," *CNN.com/U.S.,* 1 August 2003. http://news.code wind.com/go%2C7172?tn=57bcdaac7ac35641f5c7c21eb b822df7 (accessed 19 December 2003).

4. These character traits are the product of Character Counts, a nonprofit, nonpartisan, nonsectarian coalition of schools, communities, and nonprofit organizations working to advance character education by teaching the Six Pillars of Character: trustworthiness, respect, responsibility, fairness, caring, and citizenship. See http://www.charactercounts.org (accessed 19 December 2003).

5. George Barna, "Americans Are Most Likely to Base Truth on Feelings," *Barna Research Online*, 12 February 2002. http://www.barna.org/cgi-bin/PagePressRelease.asp?PressReleaseID=106&Reference=B (accessed 19 December 2003).

6. George Barna, "Practical Outcomes Replace Biblical Principles as the Moral Standard," *Barna Research Online*, 10 September 2001. http://www.barna.org/cgi-bin/PagePressRelease.asp?PressReleaseID=97&Reference=B (accessed 19 December 2003).

7. George Barna, "Most Americans Are Concerned About the Nation's Moral Condition," *Barna Research Online*, 30 April 2001. http://www.barna.org/cgi-bin/PagePressRelease.asp?PressReleaseID=89 & Reverence=B (accessed 19 December 2003).

8. The case of Alabama Supreme Court Chief Justice Roy Moore is classic. He refused to remove a Ten Commandments monument from the rotunda of the state judicial building, asserting that to do so would deny the connection with God that the state constitution was based upon. Judge Moore said, "I must acknowledge

God. That's what this case is about." U.S. District Judge Myron Thompson ordered the monument removed under the guise of the mythical "separation of church and state" constitutional requirement.

9. This is often the case in debates such as the one that raged over the qualification of Rev. Gene Robinson to become Bishop of the Episcopal Diocese of New Hampshire. Gay theologians argue that the term *detestable* or *abomination* in Leviticus 18:22 is associated with the Canaanite religious practice of cult prostitution and that what is being condemned here is idolatry, not homosexuality. They argue that God did not prohibit the kind of homosexuality we see today. But such is not the case. Proverbs 6:16–19 describes seven things that the Lord God finds detestable, and none of them relates to idolatry. If the practices condemned in Leviticus 18 and 20 are condemned only when practiced in association with idolatry, the logical conclusion is that as long as incest, adultery, bestiality, and child sacrifice (all condemned in these passages along with homosexuality) are practiced apart from idolatry, they too are acceptable. Even the gay community wouldn't try to make such a ridiculous argument.

10. By appealing to Jesus' teaching that we are to love one another, even our enemies (Matthew 5:43–44; 22:37–39), some misapply this principle. They ask, "Didn't Jesus teach that we are not to judge one another?" (Matthew 7:1–2). But in His teaching on

divorce, Jesus clearly reiterated the biblical morality of a man and a woman becoming one flesh, not a man and a man (Matthew 19:4–6). Perhaps it was the selective application of scriptural truth, evidenced in the Bishop Robinson debate, that prompted Rev. Todd H. Wetzel, executive director of Episcopalians United, to comment:

> Several years ago, I called the Rev. Gene Robinson "the most dangerous man in the Episcopal Church." I did so, not because Canon Robinson was inept or because he was lacking in compassion.... Were it not for the fact that he is engaged in an immoral lifestyle and openly displays his commitment to another man, he would in all other areas be qualified, [but] exemplary capabilities do not warrant an exception to 2000 years of the teaching of Scripture.

Al Dobras, "Episcopalians Elect Divorced, 'Gay' Bishop in New Hampshire," *Concerned Women for America*, 11 June 2003. http://www.cwfa.org/articledisplay.asp?id=4102&department=CFI&categoryid=cfreport (accessed 19 December 2003).

11. *Mr. Holland's Opus* is rated PG for profanity and vulgarity, qualities that are not commendable. *Mr. Holland's Opus* (Hollywood Pictures, 1995), rated PG, written by Patrick Sheane Duncan, directed by Stephen Herek.

12. Proverbs 6:16; Isaiah 61:8; Amos 5:21; 6:8; Zechariah
    8:17; Revelation 2:6.

Chapter Ten

1. A resource to see how Bible history intersects and
   overlaps with world history is a website called "The
   Amazing Bible World History Timeline." It gives you a
   quick, organized way to see history from Adam to
   modern times. You see the relationship between events
   which helps you have a fuller understanding of your
   Bible and world history. For more information go to
   http://www.agards.com/bible-study.

Chapter Eleven

1. F. F. Bruce, *The New Testament Documents: Are They
   Reliable?* 5th ed., rev. (Downers Grove, IL: InterVarsity
   Press, 1960).
2. Geisler and Nix comment:

   > When a comparison is made of the variant
   > readings of the New Testament with those of
   > other books which have survived from antiq-
   > uity, the results are little short of astounding.
   > For instance, although there are some
   > 200,000 "errors" among the New Testament
   > manuscripts, these appear in only about
   > 10,000 places, and only about one-sixtieth
   > rise above the level of trivialities. Westcott and
   > Hort, Ezra Abbot, Philip Schaff, and A. T.

Robertson have carefully evaluated the evidence and have concluded that the New Testament text is over 99 percent pure. In the light of the fact that there are over 5,000 Greek manuscripts, some 9,000 versions and translations, the evidence for the integrity of the New Testament is beyond question.

Norman L. Geisler and William E. Nix, *From God to Us: How We Got Our Bible* (Chicago: Moody Press, 1974).

3. Heather E. Blatt, "Letters in Late Antiquity, the Middle Ages and Renaissance," *Compleat Anachronist*, Fall 2001. http://www.people.cornell.edu/pages/heb4/letters.html (accessed 9 January 2004).

4. Heather E. Blatt, "Letters in Late Antiquity, the Middle Ages and Renaissance."

5. For more on letter writing in the Greco-Roman world, see: Carol Dana Lanham, *Salutatio Formulas in Latin Letters to 1200: Syntax, Style, and Theory* (Munchen, Germany: Arbeo-Gesellschaft, 1975), 7–22, 69–75; John L. White, *Light from Ancient Letters* (Philadelphia, PA: Fortress Press, 1986), 193–213; M. Luther Stirewalt, *Paul, the Letter Writer* (Grand Rapids, MI: Eerdmans Publishing Co., 2003).

6. One of the arguments against Pauline authorship of Hebrews is that the book of Hebrews varies so greatly from the unvaried style of Paul in his thirteen recognized epistles. Missing are most of the features discussed in this section identifying how closely Paul's writing style is to that of others during the Roman period.

7. In the Pastoral Epistles (1 Timothy, 2 Timothy, and Titus [KJV, NKJV]), Paul adds "mercy" to his traditional "grace and peace" greeting.

8. See 2 Kings 18:19–25; Ezra 4:9–16; and Esther 8:5–10.

Chapter Twelve

1. The first person to put me onto the fact that you can find Jesus in any book of the Bible you read if you only look for Him with the eyes of faith was Dr. M. L. Lowe. Dr. Lowe was one of my Bible teachers when I attended Practical Bible Training School (now Practical Bible College) in the early 60s. He wrote a book entitled *Christ in All the Scriptures,* and it opened to me the possibility that Jesus was Himself the central figure of the Bible, not just the New Testament.

2. Matthew Henry, *Matthew Henry's Commentary, Vol. V* (New York: Fleming H. Revell, Co., 1838).

3. W. A. Criswell, *The Scarlet Thread Through the Bible* (Nashville, TN: Broadman Press, 1970). Another classic treatment of the same subject is J. Sidlow Baxter's *The Master Theme of the Bible* (Grand Rapids, MI: Kregel Publications, 1997).

4. W. A. Criswell, *The Scarlet Thread Through the Bible*, 23.

Chapter Thirteen

1. George Gallup Jr. and Jim Castelli, *The People's Religion* (New York: Macmillan Publishing Company, 1989), 60.

2. George Barna, "Annual Survey of America's Faith," *Barna Research Online*, March 8, 1999. Contact Barna Research Online for further information and access to archived material.

3. George Barna, "Barna Identifies Seven Paradoxes Regarding America's Faith," *Barna Research Online*, 17 December 2002. http://www.barna.org/cgi-bin/PagePressRelease.asp?PressReleaseID=128&Reference=B (accessed 19 December 2003).

4. See Woodrow Kroll, *Read Your Bible One Book at a Time* (Ann Arbor, MI: Vine Books, 2002) for a detailed account of how long it takes to read each book of the Bible, and what to look for when you read each book.

5. Only verses 84, 90, 121, 122, and 132 do not contain either a direct or indirect reference to God's Word. Verses 57, 103, 130, and 139 refer to His "words," which also may not refer to the Bible.

6. The word *heed,* or *be careful* (Hebrew *shamar*), is found in verses 4, 5, 8, 9, 17, 34, 44, 55, 57, 60, 63, 67, 88, 101, 106, 134, 136, 146, 158, 167, and 168.

7. The word is *lamad* in Hebrew and means "to exercise" or "to drill" a student so as to help him or her learn. See verses 7, 12, 26, 64, 66, 68, 71, 73, 99, 108, 124, 135, and 171.

8. *Merriam-Webster's Collegiate Dictionary, Eleventh Ed.* (Springfield, MA: Merriam-Webster Inc. Publishers, 2003).

Epilogue

1. C. S. Lewis, *Reflections on the Psalms* (New York: Harcourt, Brace, Jovanovich, 1958), 50.